"**This* is one of the strategies I recommend in my book. Taking advantage of Time Value Premium is the most conservative option strategy, and one, which has a very high likelihood of resulting in a profit over the long term. If this is the strategy carefully followed I can endorse it**."

Mervyn L. Hecht, Author: ***How to Make Money with Stock Options: A Basic Guide for the Conservative Investor***, (Invinoveritas Press. Santa Monica, CA 2005. 3rd edition).

*   *   *   *   *   *   *   *   *

*referring to:

Ascent Option Spreads' Diagonal Put strategy is primarily:

"We buy longer term Out-of-The-Money (OTM) puts as a hedge (3 to 5 months). And, we sell over-valued short term Out-of-The-Money (OTM) or, At-The-Money (ATM) puts to earn the time premium, that will erode (to our benefit) day-by-day, as time approaches expiration. Thereby creating more credits than debits which translates into bottom-line profits."
Don Shapray (CEO, Ascent Option Spreads)

*   *   *   *   *   *   *   *   *

Testimonials

Here is what *Ascent Option Spreads* subscribers are saying in 2008:

"Don -I've been working with you and your firm since the 1st of January 2008. Your strategy intrigued me since I had not seen or read anything about a long term hedged Put Strategy. In retrospect, there was probably not a worse time to try something like this than the First Quarter of this year. I've attached a spreadsheet of my results to date. I'm not currently using TOS (Thinkorswim.com) and their Auto-trade feature. Several of my fills have been less than optimal. I've endured missed keystrokes and assorted input errors. I've been assigned 5 times. Twice on the same stock!

I anticipated a 60 through 90 day period of incurring net debits and that is exactly what occurred. The credits are starting to roll in and I'm pleased I stuck with the program. This market has been a challenge for virtually any strategy someone tried to employ. Your program works. I'm pleased enough that I'm going to be increasing the number of contracts I trade in the near future. That was part of my business plan if I was on budget, which I am.

Your service, particularly your availability to answer questions is a real asset. As the overall market improves, I can see your hedged Put plan really taking off. It's a great steady source of income.

See you in a few weeks" ---- **Robert "Bob" Shipp**, *from* **Litchfield, CT**

*　　*　　*　　*　　*　　*　　*　　*

"Don… I think the trick to your success is hard work and a great game plan. You stay **very** diversified among many great companies, you enter the market when the company seems cheap, you try and capture time premium by shorting the put and you hedge against an unexpected downturn by buying long term puts. It's a great concept that works so well over time for anyone looking to achieve an above average return on their money with protection against large draw downs and sleepless nights. Your services are unique amongst options trading systems at a cost that is fractional compared to the amount of time and energy you personally commit to making your subscribers successful! Booyah! ---- **Mark J.** *from* **Oxnard, CA**

*　　*　　*　　*　　*　　*　　*　　*　　*

Testimonials

Here is what others have to say:

"Hi Don…While it's still too early to be definitive, the consistency I've seen from your results over the past 4 years would suggest that you're better than most long traders, while between you and the other short traders, there's daylight. Regards." **Shyam** of **Pro-Option-Profits.com**

*   *   *   *   *   *   *   *   *

*"As far as other advisories, no one compares.
You are the best that I have seen."*   **Alex B**.

*   *   *   *   *   *   *   *   *

- Thanks a lot I look forward to a year of profitable (options) trading."
Jeff P.

*   *   *   *   *   *   *   *   *

- HI DON, I AM CURRENTLY AROUND 21% RETURN... I SUBSCRIBE TO BERNIE SHAFFER AND HAVE BEEN PLAYING SOME OF THEIR PICKS IN THE PLAYERS SPOTLIGHT SERIES, BUT HAVE QUIT DUE TO EXCESSIVE LOSSES. I AM FOCUSING ON YOUR STRATEGY ALONE AT THIS TIME. FOR MY OBJECTIVES, I PREFER A STEADY, POSITIVE RETURN AS OPPOSED TO TRYING TO HIT THE BIG ONE. KEEP UP THE GOOD WORK. "
Robert K.

*   *   *   *   *   *   *   *   *

- I am very impressed… you have a great service… Thank you very much!"
Elise T.

*   *   *   *   *   *   *   *   *

Testimonials

- I was told from a friend of mine that when all of their other investments were going down that their investments with Don were up over 400%. I knew that I needed to get a hold of this person. I had been praying for a service such as his. The rate of returns, are phenomenal. The integrity and price of the service are beyond compare. The rates of returns are so exciting that it's hard not to get in to every trade. My account continues to grow!! I highly recommend this service. There are many more expensive services out there with not even half of the results. " **Tina M.**

*   *   *   *   *   *   *   *   *

- Dear Don, I wanted to tell you that I have been trading some and also tracking all of your recommendations since early October [2000] when I subscribed to your service --- a tough market, to be sure. I have been very impressed with my results and with the timely email updates from you on many of your recommended stocks. For these reasons, I intend to subscribe to your service for the next year. Thank you for being there." **Terry R.**

*   *   *   *   *   *   *   *   *

- Don, I want to congratulate and thank you. With the market generally going down since my subscription started in May, until the recent bottoming (hopefully, but I doubt it), you have been able to find stocks that have actually gone up in value over this time period. Keep up the good work." **Ben M.**

*   *   *   *   *   *   *   *   *

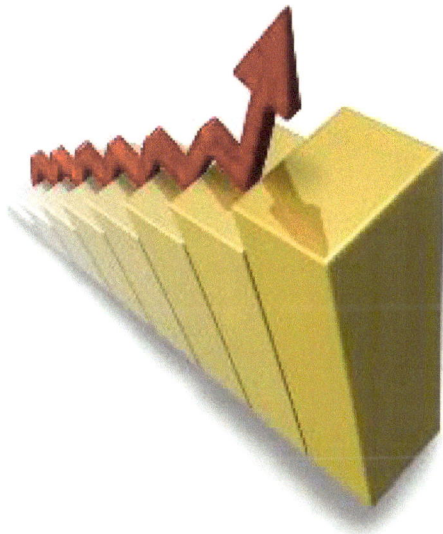

Anxiety Free Option Investing

Using Covered Spreads as a Hedge vs. Downside Risk

By

Don Shapray

and

Paul G. Ellsworth

This publication is designed to provide accurate and authoritative information in regard to the subject matter covered. It is published with the understanding that the publisher and author are not engaged in rendering legal accounting or other professional service. If legal advice or other professional advice, including financial, is required, the services of a competent professional person should be sought--- From a Declaration of Principles, jointly adopted by a Committee of the American Bar Association and a Committee of Publishers.

First Edition Published in the United States of America by Jade Emperor Publishing, PO Box 51541, Jacksonville Beach, FL 32240-1541. email: jade_emperor2000@yahoo.com

Library of Congress Cataloging-in-Publication Data:
Shapray, Don. Ellsworth, Paul G.
     Anxiety-Free Option Investing / by Don Shapray and Paul G. Ellsworth.
Includes index.
     1. Stocks – United States – Handbooks, manuals, etc. 2. Stock Options – United States – Handbooks, manuals, etc. 3. Investments. 4. Investing Strategies. 5. Finance, Personal. 6. Stock Options. 7. Stocks. 8. Stock Options Trading. 9. Option Spreads. 10. Option Spread Trading. 11. Calendar Spreads. 12. Diagonal Put Spreads. 13. Option Trading Strategies. 14. Portfolio Protection. I. Shapray, Don. II. Ellsworth, Paul G. III. Title.
ISBN 978-0-971000-33-9
Arrow Graph Image is a copyrighted image of Don Shapray & Ascent Option Spreads
Cover Design: Paul G. Ellsworth

It is **not** the intention of the author or publisher to discourage any readers from ***enjoying and benefiting from the material and strategies put forth in this publication***.

Warning – Disclaimer

However, due to the legalities of this society, this disclaimer is necessary. This book presents information and techniques that have been in use for many years. These practices, strategies and financial ideas utilize concepts within the financial investment world. However, there are no claims to effectiveness. The information offered is valid to the author's best knowledge and experience. This information is to be used by the reader(s) at their own discretion and liability. You need to accept legal responsibility for doing a thing you do not thoroughly understand. Because people's lives have different conditions and different stages of growth, no rigid or strict practice can be applied universally. The adoption and application of the material offered in this book is totally your own responsibility.

This book contains the authors' opinions. Some material in this book may be affected by changes in market conditions, or financial investment law, or the tax code (or changes in interpretations of the law or tax code). Hence, the accuracy and completeness of the information contained in this book cannot be guaranteed. Neither the author nor the publisher is engaged in rendering investment, legal, tax, accounting, or other similar professional services. If these services are required, the reader should obtain them from a competent professional.

The authors and publisher of this material are NOT RESPONSIBLE in any manner for any loss, or injury, financial or otherwise, which may occur through reading or following the instructions in this material. The strategies, financial activities and suggestions described in this material may be too risky and/or dangerous for some people, and the reader should consider the risks before applying any strategies put forth in this book. The reader may need to consult with a financial advisor for any tax implications due to the practice of any trade activity.

Table of Contents

Testimonials   3
Copyright   10
Warning – Disclaimer   11
Acknowledgements   15
Foreword   19
Preface   21
Introduction   23

The Single Most Effective System   27

SECTION 1:   *Introduction to Options*

    Chapter 1:   Options Get a Bad Rap   29
    Chapter 2:   First Protect Your Investment   31
    Chapter 3:   Risk   33
    Chapter 4:   Risk Management   35
    Chapter 5:   What is an Option?   37
    Chapter 6:   Call Options   39
    Chapter 7:   Put Options   41
    Chapter 8:   An Option Contract   43
    Chapter 9:   Our Objective and Strategy   47
    Chapter 10:   Components of an Option   49
    Chapter 11:   Stock vs. Option Purchasing   51
    Chapter 12:   Determining the Value of Options   55
    Chapter 13:   Picking Appropriate Stock Candidates   59
                for Option Trading
    Chapter 14:   Determining Your Goals   65
    Chapter 15:   Selling Short   67

Table of Contents

SECTION 2:   *The Real World of Option Trading*

Chapter 16:   An Ideal Scenario   75
Chapter 17:   Trading With an Advisory Service   79
Chapter 18:   Welcome to the Real World   83
Chapter 19:   Margin – How Does It Really Work?   91
Chapter 20:   Option Profitability Trade Log   101
Chapter 21:   Maximizing Profit on Each Trade   117
Chapter 22:   Spread Option Trades   119
Chapter 23:   Making Live Trades   125
Chapter 24:   About Ascent Option Spreads   131
Chapter 25:   Option Strategies   135

Appendix 1:   Basics of Option Trading   141
Appendix 2:   Definitions of Terms   152
Appendix 3:   Graphs of Common Movements   156
Appendix 4:   2007 Year Performance Track Record   160
Appendix 5:   2008 Year Performance Track Record   179

Index   183
About Don Shapray, Author   185
About Paul G. Ellsworth, Author   187

Acknowledgements

I simply want to thank Paul G. Ellsworth, Jade Emperor Publishing for encouraging me to formally publish this book. Paul's technical writing skills and expertise, and marketing abilities are greatly appreciated. I have given him authorization to distribute this publication on my behalf. However, after working with Paul, and his involvement with the creation of this book, I later asked that Paul co-author this book with me.

All the written concepts and materials are mine based upon years of experience within the Stock Options Investment field.

I sincerely hope that you, the reader, will find financial success beyond your highest desires through the use of the suggested strategies in this book.

To new heights,

Don Shapray
CEO, Ascent Option Spreads.

"If you do what you've always done, you'll get what you've always got."

"Winners act with experienced teachers and losers rush in without an education."

Foreword

It is with great pleasure that I write this forward for Don Shapray, CEO Ascent Option Spreads.

Don is like a seasoned navigator of deep waters. Mere sailors know how to handle the ropes and the rudder…But, the navigator needs to know how to chart through the oceans using constellations, compasses, charts, graphs, and working with the sailing vessel…while in actual motion. That is while at sea, regardless of the weather conditions; under the sun or moon; or on a cloudy or starry night.

In this way, Mr. Shapray works in conjunction with the graphs, telltale signs of a stock using opposing positions, and strategies.

He is like a maestro of a symphony that while the musical composition is already written, he draws out of the musicians (Ascent Option Spreads' analysts, educators, and worldwide licensees) a wonderful blend of what can be done within that song (stock) drawing out its finest blends and sounds (stock option strategies) breathing into it life (hopefully stock profits)… such that the audience (investor) truly benefits from his fine gestures. (strategic suggestions).

As I read this book, I felt that Don needed to seek further distribution as his advice on this sometimes misunderstood topic matter is greatly needed. Recently, Thomson Reuters (a division of the highly respected Reuters Financial News Service) confirmed my opinion by seeking Don Shapray (and Ascent Option Spreads) out as a *Partner* and *Option Spread Educator* for their worldwide established paying clientele. (For further information visit: www.equis.com and select: "partners".)

I firmly believe that no one else has such a complete understanding of these strategies, or can better advise how to use them to make money. As in many instances, success depends not only on the strategies themselves, but on how, and when, to apply them. Personally, I put considerable trust in an advisor's own track record. *Ascent Option Spreads'* track record is available on their website: **www.800option.com**, and is open for all to inspect. They are proud of it, and rightfully so. We strongly recommend that you keep track of your trading record, as well. Past performance is an excellent indicator of how you are doing… and how we are doing.

Wishing you the best of success in all of your financial and personal endeavors, and hoping that, perhaps, this material will assist you in attaining heightened investing skills and strategic techniques, specifically with regards to stock options trading and investing.

Kind regards,

Paul G. Ellsworth
CEO, Jade Emperor Publishing

PREFACE

How to Make Money with Stock Options: A Basic Guide for the Conservative Investor, (Invinoveritas Press. Santa Monica, CA 2005. 3rd edition) by Mervyn L. Hecht, is an introduction for the conservative, non-professional investor to the strategies used by professional investors to increase yield on investment through the use of stock options. Beginning with the basic elements of the differences between stocks and options, Mr. Hecht gradually moves the reader to the advanced stages of option strategies, including buying and selling puts and calls, spreads, and buy-writes. Throughout his book the emphasis is on conservative strategies, and an understanding of what makes particular strategies risky or conservative (and what those terms mean). He includes practical sections on mitigation of losses and hedging, and helpful diagnoses of common psychological pitfalls that sometimes influence our decision making in the market. Finally, there are sections giving practical advice specifically to stockbrokers and lawyers handling option-related cases. **How to Make Money with Stock Options** makes this complex subject manageable for the average investor who wants to increase his or her investment return while maintaining a conservative posture.

In his book, Mr. Hecht states:

"While option strategies are not for everyone, I believe that most investors can master the basic concepts, and use them to advantage. Above all I believe that an investor who understands and uses options can invest with less risk than one who doesn't use options. "   (page 5)

We agree with this perspective, and that is one of the reasons for the writing of our book. **However, we intend to expand from this foundation by mostly covering specific option trading strategies…**

We **highly recommend** Mr. Hecht's book as a great foundational understanding of option trading and various situations. He has written an excellent book, which should be on every serious investor's bookcase or desk.

INTRODUCTION

Here is MATERIAL that you need to read AND re-read from time to time.

Stock Option Trading is Not complicated if you think of it in these terms or relate it to this. It is not technical or complicated it is TOTALLY logical if you think of it in these terms.

WHY IS OPTION-SPREAD TRADING OR WRITING SIMILAR TO BEING AN INSURANCE UNDERWRITER?

Options namely puts are insurance policies that investors purchase guaranteeing them the right but not the obligation to sell stock at a specific price for a specified period of time. **Why would someone purchase a Put? There are only 2 reasons:**

a.) Protect a profit in a stock in the hopes that it would increase in price.
b.) Fear that the stock will decline.

- **How are premiums determined?**

By, demand versus supply as in all commodities.

Psychologically clients are bearish short-term, but, bullish long-term. Hence, short-term puts become over inflated and long-term puts are under inflated because of the demand versus supply imbalance. Obviously, we wish to purchase cheap re-insurance (i.e. long Puts) to protect are over-inflated puts sold. This is what a prudent insurance underwriter would do regardless of what type insurance policies he was issuing.

- **Do you know of any insurance underwriters that lose money?**

The insurance underwriter earns premium by the passage of time to expiration of the policy. The option writer (underwriter) similarly earns premium by the passage of time to the expiration of the Put; whether the stock remains static, or rises.

We are simply taking this logic or approach and applying it to the stock market. It is counter-intuitive to sell high in advance and buy back cheaper. Most people buy low and sell high. They overlook the possible scenario, again, of sell high in advance and buy back cheaper.

As you know there is Benefit in **thinking -"outside the box"**,* in order to see the whole or complete picture. However, once that picture has been seen, then applying micro- strategies can be best utilized or served.

*An example of thinking "outside the box": Have you ever asked yourself, why are houses built in squares or rectangles and not polygons or circles? Castles (turrets) and lighthouses withstand outside forces such as hurricanes, and shifting winds with reduced risk of implosion.

FACT: Savvy insurance underwriters buy re-insurance to hedge their risk.

STRATEGY: Since it is a proven statistic that 76% + of all purchased options expire worthless, regardless of the market trend, it goes without saying that we are on the right track. **Why do we sell puts and not calls?** Psychology my friends! It is human nature to be bullish long term and bearish short term. We are optimists. How does this influence our decision-making process? Well obviously put premiums are determined by excesses of supply vs. demand. So what side of the equation do we park ourselves on? No brainer mates. We buy **"Out-of-The-Money" (OTM)** cheap longer term puts as our insurance policy or license to capture premiums from overvalued at the money short term puts.

- ## Why are the short term puts overvalued?

Because short term put buyers are bearish, short-term, so that demand exceeds supply and inflation of premium results, which we capture in our portfolios. The short term premium erodes, funneling profits into our pockets faster than the long term deterioration if the stock remains unchanged, rises slowly or falls 10%. You ask: How do I lose? If the stock falls precipitously and never recovers you can lose your debit and differential in the strike price between the long and short put. **That is why we take credits as they develop in order to mitigate the above unlikely scenario**.

- ## Do not measure your profitability of your account by looking at the net liquidating value in your broker's statement.

Why? **Because this does <u>not</u> factor in the premiums that you will capture transaction by transaction until the long put expiration date**. Be patient. Allow us to take money off the table as we do with our daily update e-mails ("a Bird in the hand is worth 2 in the Bush"). Allow us with our Platinum Plus subscription, to tighten the spread by moving up the strike price of the long put at the right time so that your net credits exceed your debits This take many hours of diligent research and careful evaluation. This procedure translates into profits obviously. **We hope that the above translates into anxiety-free option investing which has always been our *modis operendi*.**

The Single Most Effective System
For
Stock-Option Trading

This course contains many examples of this time tested trading strategy. We will stress the importance of these strategies by using repetition. Perhaps you remember how your schoolteachers repeated certain terms, or ideas, to prepare you for an upcoming test. Your test here could mean the difference between you making and losing money. Therefore, we want to ensure that you thoroughly understand the concepts contained herein.

Before anyone should consider option trading, it would be **advisable** to gather as much information on the subject as possible.

The **Security and Exchange Commission (SEC**) is the regulatory agency for **all** securities trading in the United States of America. It **requires** traders to have a basic knowledge of the stock market **before** it will allow anyone to trade options.

Every brokerage firm has its own minimum experience criteria before allowing a customer access to trading. If a trader incurs losses beyond his financial ability to cover them, the brokerage firm that actually made the trade is held responsible.

The system must guard against those who would act without obtaining the proper knowledge, expertise, or funds to do so. Do **not** put yourself into that category. Invest prudently, and intelligently. You are taking a step in obtaining this knowledge by reading this book and/or attending one of my seminars. Our goal is to help you reach that necessary level of understanding.

SECTION 1: Introduction to Options

Chapter 1: Options Get a Bad Rap

The **Option Clearing Corporation** **(OCC)** ensures there will be a buyer for every seller, and a seller for every buyer, and that all transactions are handled smoothly and fairly. This regulatory service creates stability for Options Trading, which would not be possible otherwise.

Option Trading has its own language but so does accounting, medicine, engineering, etc. Because of this new language Option Trading is generally misunderstood. Trading Options has a scary reputation. Traditionally, it is believed that the great majority of those who avoid trading in options are put off by the need to learn a specialized language in order to understand the process, and in dealing with the brokers who actually make the trades. Terms like: puts, calls, spreads, covered positions, roll-outs, naked, contracts, etc. are common enough words ,but when used within the context of Option Trading, they have slightly different meanings.

An investor needs certain tools to consistently succeed in trading securities. Among these are:

- **Knowledge**.

- **A source for accurate and timely information**.

- **An overall strategy**.

- **Self-discipline**.

- **The desire to succeed**.

- And, **the funds to make it all happen**.

The recipe requires *__all__* the ingredients. If one ingredient is missing, then the degree of success obtainable is seriously impaired.

Chapter 2: First Protect Your Investment

It almost sounds like part of the Hippocratic oath: *"First, do no harm."* Maximum protection of your investment is paramount; from the moment you make the trade, until the position is closed.

There is risk associated with virtually all types of option trading. However, you can learn to mitigate those risks by using specific option strategies. Once you learn to manage risk in any situation, the process becomes more enjoyable, and the potential rewards greater.

There are many basic differences between investors and traders. Basically, we will define them as follows:

Investor: generally intends to passively leave his investments in place for a longer period of time, through both highs and lows of market fluctuation.

Trader: tends to make shorter-term "trades", taking advantage of market highs while attempting to avoid the lows.

This book focuses on the **Trader**; more specifically the **"Stock Options" Trader**, and then, only low-risk trades that statistically are less risky than owning stocks.

We think you will join others that use this proven method – and reap its rewards.

Techniques employed by traders are generally more active and are intended to primarily make profit on the trade itself. If a trader's portfolio is truly balanced, however, it will also contain both short, as well as long-term holdings. Trading stock options is a method of using small amounts of money to make exceptionally high profits within a short period of time. Conversely, and all things being equal, you can lose the same amount of money, in the same amount of time.

Many traders open their accounts with relatively small amounts of money, between $2,000.00 and $10,000.00. The **Securities and Exchange Commission (SEC)** mandates a minimum of $2,000.00 to open an account. However, most brokerage firms have established their own required account minimums.

Practice thorough research on your subject stocks.

- Develop a solid system of operating parameters, and stick with them.
- Keep accurate accounting records.
- Set realistic goals on every trade… and overall. When your goals have been reached, take profits and move to the next opportunity.
- Be patient and develop a healthy respect for risk – Learn how to effectively manage it, or it could be your worst enemy.
- Begin with paper-trades, and then graduate to trades using small amounts of money. You will inevitably make mistakes… everyone does, so if your beginning investments are small, then your losses will be small.
- Keep a journal. There is no substitute for personal experiences, even negative ones – Learn from them.

Chapter 3: Risk

Risk is the single most frightening aspect of trading any form of securities.

Risk and reward are thought to be the parallel twins of investing. Where one goes, the other is believed to consistently travel parallel to it.

When investment risks are high, there is usually an underlying cause for the associated volatility, creating a similarly high profit potential.

When risks are low, so it seems is profit potential.

While I believe this to be generally accurate, as with any other rule in life, it has exceptions. With the method of option training taught here we have mitigated the risk while maintaining large reward.

Chapter 4: Risk Management

- **Know the risk of every trade you make.**

- **Know the limits of every trade you make. (Acceptable profits, as well as acceptable losses.)**

- **Define goals within your own parameters.**

- **Stick to your system, goals, and proven strategies, even in the face of strong temptation.**

- **Develop self-control.**

Part of the well-deserved appeal of trading stock options is that it is done with little interest in market fluctuations. You will no longer need to scour the Internet while simultaneously keeping one ear tuned to CNBC for any scrap of news that could potentially mean disaster, or opportunity, to your life savings. Using the strategies contained within this book, you will be able to enjoy a methodical, low stress system of risk management trading. We advocate adding to your leisure time, not your stress level.

This option trading method:

- Doesn't matter whether we are in a bull or bear market.
- Delivers 30% to 60% earnings, and sometimes more!
- Performance with less risk than owning stock.

This is not some mystifying secret or voodoo. But, **a basic system of risk management coupled with a specific option strategy**.

Chapter 5: What is an Option?

An ***option*** is a contract providing its owner with:

- **The right, but _not_ the obligation, to buy or sell something of value**
- **At a specified, fixed price (the striking price), and**
- **By a predetermined date (the expiration date).**

If you have never read the definition of an option before, it will be repeated many times within the following pages.

When you purchase an option, you do not buy stocks, bonds, or any other tangible asset. You are purchasing the "right" to buy or sell that asset at a specified, fixed price (the striking price), and you must make that transaction by a predetermined date in the future, or the option will expire, worthless.

At first glance, the wisdom of such a transaction seems questionable, but contained within the option concept lies tremendous opportunity.

There are two types of options:

Calls, and Puts.

- ***Call*** = means that you want to "Call-in",

    <u>Buy</u>   the right to purchase an item of value, which is the basis of the option, or

    <u>Sell</u>   the right to someone else to buy it from you.

- ***Put*** = means you want to "Put" the item to someone else,

    <u>Sell</u>   them the right to sell the item to you or

    <u>Buy</u>   the right to sell an item of value to someone else.

Chapter 6: Call Options

Let's look at the following examples.

Example 1:
Perhaps at some point in your life, you have purchased an item on a layaway plan. You make an initial payment toward the full price of that item and are guaranteed to be able to complete the purchase within an agreed upon time limit, and at the fixed price at the time of layaway. Sound familiar?

You bought a Call option!!

If you decide to complete the purchase by the predetermined expiration date, then you are ***exercising*** your option.

If not, then you lose whatever money you originally paid to hold the item, and the seller is no longer obligated to produce the item at the agreed upon price.

When you ***buy*** an option, you pay money to someone else for the right to control the disposition of the underlying item of value. At anytime before the expiration date of your option, the store is obligated to make the item available to you at the agreed upon price. <u>Please understand this concept thoroughly</u>, as it will play a central part in our future strategies.

- **The buyer of an option has rights, and**

<u>Pays</u> **a premium for them.**

- **The seller of an option has obligations, and**

<u>Receives</u> **a premium to assume them.**

Example 2:   It is June of this year, and you have a lease on your current residence. It is a nice house, and you feel it would be a good buy at today's market price. However, because of employment uncertainties you don't want to make the actual commitment to buy the house until next Spring. The owner of the house has indicated that the house is for sale for $100,000, and you are concerned that he might sell the house before you have the

opportunity to make an offer. You approach the owner of the property and suggest the following:

> **You agree to pay him $1,000.00 for the *right*,**
>
> **But *not* the obligation,**
>
> **to purchase the house for $100,000.00 (the striking price),**
>
> **today's Market Value, sometime between now,**
>
> **and May of next year (the expiration date).**

The property owner has nothing to lose. He will be earning $1,000.00 by granting your right to purchase the house at a later date, but at today's locked-in, market price. Meanwhile, property values could rise, but they could also fall. He thinks they might fall, and if so, he could still have a willing buyer for his house without having to list the house with a realtor, thereby saving him a commission on the sale. If property values rise during that period, he could lose the increased value of the property, but it is worth the gamble.

By making this agreement, you have <u>purchased a Call option.</u>

In our example illustrated above:

- You are the **"buyer"** of the option. You have the ***right to exercise*** that option at any time before the predetermined, expiration date, and at the specified price.

- The Property Owner is the **"seller"** of the option. He is ***obligated*** to make the property available to you at any time before expiration, and at the specified price.

Chapter 7: Put Options

A "***Put***" **option** can be used to accomplish the same result as a "***Call***" **option**, but <u>disposition of the property is reversed</u>.

- A <u>**Put**</u> **option** grants the owner the right to ***sell*** an item of value at a specified, fixed price, and by a predetermined date in the future.

Just like the ***Call*** option, the ***buyer* of a *Put*** option must pay for the privilege of having control over the disposition of the item of value. A ***Put*** option grants its owner the right, but not the obligation to *sell* an item of value at a specified, fixed price, and by a predetermined date in the future.

If the option is <u>**not**</u> exercised by the specified, expiration date, it expires, worthless.

Chapter 8: An Option Contract

<u>There are six basic components to an option contract</u>:

1. Determining whether you want to buy or sell the option.
2. Description of the type of option. (Call or Put.)
3. Description of the item of value. (House, car, stocks, real estate, etc.)
4. The striking price of that item of value. (The specified, fixed price for which you want to buy or sell the item of value, sometime in the future.)
5. The expiration date of the option, after which, the option becomes worthless.
6. The price the buyer will pay to the seller for the option.

Look at the following example:

> I make miniature sailboats for sale to a major retailer. My wholesale price for each boat is $200.00, while the retailer sells them for $300.00. Since I can sometimes sell my boats out of my house for $250.00, I don't want to obligate my entire inventory exclusively to the retailer. But, at the same time I need a ready, retail market for my product.

In order to stabilize my market, I *purchase* a "**<u>Put</u>**" option from my retailer.

- I agree to pay him $50.00 for the right, but ***not*** the obligation, to sell him any number of sailboats that I can produce until the first of next year, and at the $200.00 wholesale price.

This agreement ensures a ready, retail market for my merchandise and guards against the retailer finding another boat-maker to replace my product. Control over the guaranteed sale of my boats costs me a premium of $50.00, and is certainly worth the security it buys. It acts like an insurance policy, of sorts. The retailer is happy with the $50.00 he's earned while securing a steady source for his inventory.

- I purchased (bought) a "**_Put_**" option, or the right, but **_not_** the obligation, to sell an item of value at a specified, fixed price, and by a predetermined date in the future.

You can place yourself in the position of being:

- The Call buyer

- The Call seller

- The Put buyer

- The Put seller

Example 3: Golf Course Real Estate

Consider the following scenario:

On our daily drive to work, we notice a new and unusually beautiful golf course along the highway. We believe there is an excellent opportunity for someone to purchase the land around the golf course and re-sell it as building lots. The owner wants one million dollars ($1,000,000.00) for just over 40 acres, or $25,000 per acre. We are fairly certain we can sell lots of one acre for $50,000, which would generate two million dollars ($2,000,000.00), which would be a 100% profit. Even after basically developing the land, we could easily profit by $600,000.

Logic dictates that we first purchase the land for one million dollars ($1,000,000.00), then develop and re-sell it in smaller, individual parcels. Alas, we do not have, nor can you acquire, the capital needed to make the purchase. Instead, we approach the property owner with an offer to **_purchase a Call option_**. We agree to pay him a $30,000 premium for the option to buy the 40 acres for one million dollars, sometime within one year. We explain to him that he keeps the $30,000 in any event - whether or not the option is exercised. He agrees.

We then proceed to get commitments from perspective buyers to purchase the one-acre lots for $50,000 each. The first month we only find 4 people willing to commit to buying the lots. But, as people sign on, others soon follow. During the second and third months, 10 people sign up, and 10 more sign up during the fourth and fifth months. So far we have a total commitment of one million two hundred thousand dollars ($1,200,000.00). We set up a meeting at our title company to ***exercise our option to simultaneously buy the land, and then sell the lots, in one transaction***. In effect, we have used other people's money to finance the purchase. Any other lots we sell will be mostly profit, and we have only sold 24 out of a potential of 40.

- **Now, replace the items of value in the above examples with stocks.**

We are allowed to buy and sell stock-options through our brokerage firms and assume either side of the transaction we wish.

Most stock options are bought and sold in lots of 100 shares, called "contracts".

If we **buy a Call option** for one contract of ABC stock, we **buy the right to buy** 100 shares of ABC stock at a specified, fixed price (the striking price), until a predetermined expiration date.

The **strategy** outlined above in Example 3 is **to purchase a long-term option on an item of value, then partially finance that purchase by selling shorter-term options on the same item of value.**

Chapter 9: Our Objective and Strategy

Our Objective:

We use other people's money to make handsome profits for ourselves.

The above example is a generalization. But, the strategic concept applies. Substitute stock options for the building lots, and see the intrinsic logic within.

Purchase a put option with an expiration date 5 to 6 months in the future.

Then sell successive, shorter-term put options on the same stock, each expiring in the nearest month.

The long-term option acts as a continuous hedge in reducing the risks associated with the sale of the successive short options.

To the unfamiliar, some of the terms used in option trading might seem a bit unusual. However, through examples and explanation you will soon become familiar with this unique terminology.

When you *sell* a stock-option, you receive money from the buyer because you are relinquishing control over the disposition of that stock, while assuming the obligation to either buy, or sell, that stock at the option of the buyer.

<u>**Options are not offered on all stocks**</u>, only those that meet criteria set by the options exchanges. Since the exchanges have agreed to act as a buyer to all sellers, and a seller to all buyers, there must be an ongoing demand for those specific options. The underlying stock can be volatile enough to create fairly rapid swings in price, thereby creating a vigorous and fluid market. The underlying stock can also have a generally static value while creating speculation about its future price movement. Differing opinions (speculation) concerning price movement creates a market for options.

Chapter 10: Components of an Option

Your Intentions: What do you want to accomplish? Do you want your investment to rise and fall with the price of the underlying stock? Perhaps you don't want to be concerned with the rise and fall of stock prices at all. But, simply make money on the trade itself.

No. of Contracts: How many option contracts do you want to trade? Most contracts contain 100 shares of stock, and must be bought or sold in those multiples.

Stock Name: You should know the name of the company, as well as its stock symbol.

Strike Price: The striking price is the specified, fixed price of the underlying stock to be bought or sold in the event of the exercise of the option.

Expiration Date: (X Date). The expiration date is specified within the option agreement, before which, the option can be exercised, and after which, the option expires, worthless. The actual expiration date is the 3rd Saturday in the expiration month. Since there is currently no trading on Saturdays, all trading must be completed by market close on the previous Friday. The actual time that expiration is made on a contract varies by broker. You should know when your broker exercises your options.

When you buy or sell a stock-option contract through a broker, your side of the transaction is automatically matched with an opposing transaction from another trader. That person will remain anonymous, and you should not be concerned about the buyer/seller's identity. *The Options Exchange acts as both, your opposing buyer, or seller, and then proceeds to match transactions.*

Cost of Option: The prices of all options are listed on the four options exchanges. Among those available is the **Chicago Board of Options Exchange (CBOE)**, which can be accessed through the Internet at www.CBOE.com From that website, all options available for trade are listed by expiration month, and the data are constantly being upgraded throughout the trading day. Both "**Bid**" and "**Ask**" prices are categorized for easy access. We do not recommend trading at "**Market**" prices; rather prefer to tilt the offers in our favor. If you trade several contracts in one transaction, the savings by using "**Limit**" orders could be substantial, depending upon your brokerage. We will go into more detail concerning actual option trading in later pages. (This is where yard sale bartering expertise might come in handy.)

Chapter 11: Stock vs. Option Purchasing

The difference between purchasing stock, or purchasing a call option instead.

(Brokerage fees vary widely; therefore they will not be considered here)

Stock investors occasionally prefer to purchase a *Call* option instead of paying full price for a stock outright.

In buying a *Call* option instead of the stock, the option buyer's investment is a fraction of the stock's face value, plus,

If the stock were to fall in price, the *Call* option buyer's losses would be limited to the price he paid for the option.

Example: ABCD stock price is $60.00

We purchase a call option –

for 4, ($4.00 per share X 100 shares = $400.00, and with a strike price of $60.00. We have bought the right to purchase 100 shares of the underlying stock for $60.00 per share anytime before expiration of the option. On the expiration date of the option, the stock price has fallen to $50.00 per share. We lose the entire premium of $400.00 we paid for the option. If we had purchased 100 shares of the same stock and paid the face value of $6,000.00, we would have lost $1,000.00. Compared to purchasing the stock outright, we managed our risk very well indeed. When we purchase a call option we expect the underlying stock price to rise, or else we would not have bought the option.

In the above example, the underlying stock moved in the opposite direction than we expected.

Example:

ABC Stock is selling for $50.00 per share. Jim will purchase the stock outright while we will purchase a **Call** option for the same amount of shares of the same stock. The abbreviated option purchase would look something like the following:

Buy one contract of ABC stock, September 50 calls for 4.

Translation:

We are buying one option contract (100 shares) of ABC stock. The option expires on the 3ʳᵈ Saturday in September, at a fixed price of $50.00 per share. The option premium we pay is $4.00 per share, or $4.00 x 100 shares = $400.00. For the $400.00 premium, we have the right to buy 100 shares of ABC stock at any time before the 3ʳᵈ Saturday in September for $50.00 per share, regardless of the actual share price at the time. We think the stock price will rise and are willing to pay the premium for the option. Our cost $400.00.

Jim paid full price for buying 100 shares of ABC stock $50.00 per share x 100 = $5000.00.

We bought one contract (100 shares) of ABC Call option with a strike price of $50.00, for 4.

4 x 100 shares = $400.00.

We both control 100 shares of ABC stock.

If the stock price rises 10 points, to $60.00 per share, the owner of the stock earns $1,000.00. $10.00 x 100 shares = $1,000.00.

The owner of the option has purchased the right to **buy** 100 shares of ABC stock at the striking price of $50.00 per share. If he wishes to exercise his option, he can buy the 100 shares of ABC stock for $50.00 per share and simultaneously sell them for $60.00 per share, earning the same $1,000.00. However, the option owner would also lose the premium of $400.00 he originally paid for the option. $1,000.00 – $400.00 = $600.00 net profit. We can view the $400.00 option premium in two ways: It acts as a hedge in allowing us to determine which way the stock price will move *before* actually purchasing the stock at the lower strike price. Also, it acts as insurance in the event the stock price falls, instead of rising. If it does fall, we simply do not exercise our option to buy the stock. Whether or not we exercise our option, we forfeit the option premium.

If we have a gain on our trade, we must consider the expenditure of the option premium as an expense and subtract it from our gains for a *net* profit. In the above instance, owning the option will prevent us from incurring a loss in the trade. But, the option premium we paid is also an expense.

If the stock falls from $50.00 per share to $40.00 per share, Jim, who owned the stock, would lose $1,000.00. The owner of the option would not exercise it, but would allow it to expire. His only loss would be the $400.00 premium he paid for the option.

The owner of the stock has unlimited upside potential, while also having equally unlimited downside risk. The owner of the *Call* option has unlimited upside potential, while having very limited downside risk, or the cost of the option. Both have the right to control 100 shares of ABC stock. But, the option owner has managed his risk far better than the stockowner while retaining all of the stock's upside earning potential. The main advantage a call buyer enjoys, over a stock buyer is that he does not have to tie up large sums of money buying stocks in order to control them. The major disadvantage for the call option buyer is that the option must become valuable and move to a position where it can be exercised at a profit to its owner, or **In-The-Money (ITM)**, during a limited period of time, or the option becomes worthless.

Chapter 12: Determining the Value of Options

The following three factors determine the value of options:

- Ownership of the option – Or the right to control the disposition of the underlying stock.

- Intrinsic value of the option – Determined by whether the option is **In-The-Money (ITM)**

- Time value remaining in the option.

I. Ownership

The value of the first factor, ***ownership***, is obvious. If you are the owner, or have control over the ownership of an item – that control has value. You can then buy it, sell it, or allow its value to decay… it's your option. However, as we will explore in later pages, value lies not only in ownership, but, also in how you can use that ownership to your best and continuous advantage, using combination strategies of put and call options.

II. Intrinsic Value

In January, Jason bought a call option on ABC stock with a striking price of $20.00, expiring in April, for $2.00 per share. (Bought 1 contract ABC April 20 call for 2). The stock price at the time of purchase was $17.00. The stock price being lower than the striking price of the option categorizes the call option as **Out-of-the-Money (OTM)**. The option presently has little value since Jason would not want to exercise it and purchase 100 shares of ABC stock for $20.00 per share, the striking price, when he could buy it on the open market for $17.00. But values can rapidly change. At this point all of the value of the option lies in the time remaining before expiration. Jason has three months before the option expires, worthless. That is plenty of time for the ***stock price*** to increase to above the $20.00 ***striking price***. If the stock price increases to $25.00, then Jason could exercise the option and buy 100 shares of ABC stock for $20.00 per share, then simultaneously sell them for $25.00 per share, earning $5.00 per share, or $500.00. $500.00 - $200.00 (Cost of the option) = $300.00 net profit.

When the stock price increases to above the striking price of a *Call* option, the option is **In-The-Money (ITM)** and can then be exercised for a profit. Also, with a *Call* option, the more the underlying stock price increases above the option's strike price, the more the option's intrinsic value increases, dollar by dollar. In the above example, there would be little value change in the option status as the stock price rose from $17.00 to $20.00 per share. However, as the stock price reached the same level as the strike price, both, $20.00, then any further upward movement in the stock price also would cause the option value to increase exponentially. The option would move from **OTM**, to **ATM**, and finally to **ITM**.

The option owner has the right to exercise his option anytime he chooses until the expiration date, if it is advantageous to him. If there is no advantage, he has no obligation to do so. The option owner is in total control of the option's disposition within the specified limits of the option contract. In actual practice the option will not automatically be exercised simply because it is **In-The-Money (ITM)**. Having sold an option that becomes **ITM**, you might experience the exercise immediately or perhaps not until the stated date of expiration. An option with the strike price and the stock price having the same value is said to be **At-The-Money (ATM)**.

CALL OPTIONS

- Stock price - $17.00 Striking price - $20.00. The option is **OTM**, and will <u>not</u> be exercised.

- Stock price - $25.00 Striking price - $20.00. The option is **ITM**, and **will likely** be exercised.

- Stock price - $20.00 Striking price - $20.00. The option is **ATM**, and will <u>not</u> be exercised.

The intrinsic value of a *call* option increases, point for point, after the underlying stock price increases to a greater value than the strike price.

PUT OPTIONS

Put options are opposite because they involve selling, not buying. A *Put* option is OTM when the stock price is higher than the strike price. **A *Put* option is ITM when the stock price is lower than the striking price.**

- Stock price - $17.00 Striking price - $20.00.
  The option is **ITM**, and **will likely** be exercised.

- Stock price - $25.00 Striking price - $20.00.
  The option is **OTM**, and will **not** be exercised.

- Stock price - $20.00 Striking price - $20.00.
  The option is **ATM**, and the option will **not** be exercised.

A Put option's intrinsic value increases, point for point, after the stock price decreases to a lesser value than the stock price.

When an option is ITM, its owner can exercise it for profit. Therefore, its intrinsic value is increased. With a Put option, the more the underlying stock price decreases the more intrinsic value the option enjoys. When an option is OTM it will not be exercised. Therefore, its value is decreased. **The degree of OTM or ITM is directly related to the point difference between the option's strike price and the underlying price of the stock at the time**.

III. Time Value

Another major factor that acts to vary the value of options is time. The more time remaining before an option's expiration date the more value it has. Whatever the underlying stock price, the option has a greater chance of moving to a position of ITM when there is an abundance of time for it to do so.

If your option is OTM and expires in six months, there is no real reason to be concerned. If at anytime during those six months your option moves to a position of being ITM, you can exercise it for a profit. However, if it is OTM, and expires in three days, then time is a major factor and is working against you. The closer to expiration, the less your option will be worth. That ***considered*** worth is part of the basis for pricing options by the options board. Intrinsic value and time value, along with demand and volatility, are all constantly evaluated in determining the value of options on the open market.

Chapter 13: Picking Appropriate Stock Candidates for Option Trading

When considering option purchases, or sales, you must either do extensive research on the underlying stock yourself, or rely on someone else to do it for you – Someone you trust. Many factors must be considered. Among these are:

- The stock's history and movement.
- Expected earnings reports of the stock's parent company.
- Volatility and volume of shares traded daily.
- Any current news concerning the company's growth or profitability.

The price of the option with respect to how you think the stock will perform. If you do not feel the stock's movement will handily offset the cost of the option, plus the trading fees, then buying or selling the option would be fruitless.

- Supply and demand of the underlying stock.

When you ***purchase a call*** option:

You expect the price of the underlying stock price to rise so you can then purchase it at the lower strike price, making a profit in the transaction.

You have the right to control 100 shares of stock for a fraction of the cost of purchasing the stock.

You are managing your risk by limiting the downside to the premium paid for the option. **The major downside to *buying* any option is time decay**. Your option expires within a finite period of time. If the underlying stock price behaves as expected, you will not need to be concerned about execution.

Having shown you the benefits of buying calls over the risks of purchasing the stocks outright, we must emphasize the fact that buying short-term calls has its associated risks as well. A call buyer, especially a short-term call buyer, is severely limited by the time-decay factor. The nearer to the expiration of an option, the less the option is worth, and the less time is remaining for the option to become profitable. Within the leverage used by gambling casinos (the house), the concept of short-term call buying is completely understood, as well as exploited, as gamblers are considered short-term call buyers.

Example:

The casino (the house) offers to sell you the chance to acquire great wealth by your risking a relatively small amount of money for that opportunity. As long as you continue to feed the slot machines, or ante up, that option is in force. But, time is *always* on the side of the "House". If you buy this short-term option, your time is severely limited to the time it takes for the tumblers to stop tumbling, or the last card is dealt, then you must keep repeating the process until time, and money, finally runs out. Regardless of the stacked odds, people keep right on feeding those one armed bandits, and betting on the next card. Would you rather be the "House" raking in huge profits from short-term call buyers… or the gamblers?

When you choose a stock for short-term call buying you not only must carefully consider the proper stock for the type of option you are buying, you must also decide which direction the stock will move. Then, that movement must occur within a specified, very limited period of time. Many investors have gone broke by attempting to make those same decisions. In short, time is **not** on the side of the short-term option buyer. **Time is on the side of the option seller**.

When you *sell* a *call* option:

You expect the underlying stock price to fall so the option will not be exercised, but expire, worthless. You can then capture the entire premium that was paid to you, as profit.

If the underlying stock price rises, you are obligated to sell 100 shares of stock at the lower strike price. If you do not already own those shares, you would then have to buy them at a higher market value. Then, sell them at the strike price in order to meet your obligation. This situation is called a "Naked", or "Uncovered" position, and is extremely dangerous. **Anytime you sell a call option you should consider buying the same option with a slightly lower strike price, and with the same or longer, expiration date**. This will reduce your profit potential, but will also reduce your risk considerably. (Remember the parallel twins, Risk and Reward – If you want to reduce risk, you must also give up some degree of potential rewards.)

When you *__purchase__* a *__put__* option:

You expect the price of the underlying stock to fall, allowing you to sell stock at the higher strike price, and thereby earning profit.

This option is also used in a combination strategy as a hedge against selling puts. We will explore that strategy later, in detail.

Buying put options could also be used as a hedge against the possibility of a price drop in stock you already own.

You own 100 shares of ABC stock, and are concerned that the stock price could suddenly fall. You purchase a put option on the same stock with a strike price at current market value. If your stock falls in price, you would have the right to exercise your option and sell 100 shares of ABC stock at the higher strike price. The premium you paid for the option could be far less than the loss you would have incurred without that insurance. In this instance, buying puts acted as a hedge against the possibility of a price decrease in the stocks you already own. If the price of the underlying stock increases, your loss is limited to the premium you paid for the option. The option acts as an insurance policy against possible loss.

When *__Selling__* a *__put__* option without an opposing hedge – "Naked":

You expect the price of the underlying stock to increase, causing the option to expire worthless. You can then capture the entire premium paid to you as profit.

If the underlying stock price were to fall below the strike price, then you would be obligated to purchase the stock at the strike price, or pay the difference between the strike price and the stock price, if you do not want to own the stock. Your upside is limited to the premium received for selling the option. Your downside is potentially unlimited to the base value of whatever you could sell the stock for on the open market, or to the difference between the strike price and the stock price. __This is a "Naked" or "Uncovered" position and should never be allowed to occur, unintentionally__. Without the implementation of combination strategies, the main objective of the ***put seller*** is to hope the option expires, allowing him to capture the entire option premium as profit. Nearing expiration, if the stock price moves below the strike price, making the option, **In-The-Money (ITM)** and highly vulnerable to exercise, then the option seller must move quickly to buy back the option, perhaps lessening his profit potential while also managing his risk. Even so, a small loss would be better than having to buy 100 shares of stock at inflated prices.

Real Examples:

- How can you tell if a stock will rally near term?

Compare the exact call premium Out-of-The-Money (OTM) with exact differential between the stock price and the put price differential stock versus strike. If the call premium is considerably higher, then you can bet that the stock will rally.

Example:

Looking at Stock: **VISA**, today (06-10-2008), the Stock price = 82 Sept 90 **Call** – 5.80, (**8 points OTM**),

Call premium higher Sept 75 **Put** 4.80 (**7 points OTM**).

Example:

Another example to confirm: **AAPL** 185 + 3.38.

On 06-10-2008: Oct 185 **Put** - 18.90. Oct 185 **Call** 21.20.

Quite a disparity!

This is why we prefer <u>put spreads for bullish orientation</u> rather than call spreads. Why? Because long term puts are cheaper, because the investing public is more *bullish* than *bearish* long term. Makes sense, right?

An e-mail was sent, on Tuesday, June 10, 2008 15:17pm EST, Subject: Don's stock pick #2:

Look for stocks that outperform the Dow intraday.

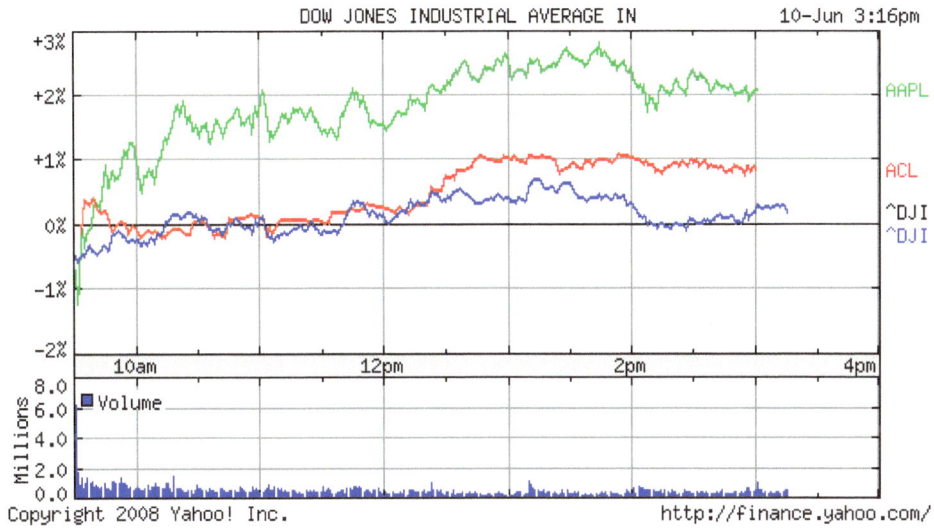

Chapter 14: Determining Your Goals

Before engaging in any type of options trading, establish your goals. What are your limits for losses and what are acceptable as gains? No matter how good a stock seems, it will occasionally slide into disfavor, and for a myriad of reasons. Even though positions on a stock have earned you a handsome profit over the last few months, the time will come when you'll want to abandon it and catch the next "Rising Star". Know when to make that move. Of course, everyone wants to maximize their profits, but in setting realistic limits on potential profits, as well as losses, you can avoid the turnaround areas of volatility... the extreme ends. This is simply another form of risk management.

There are numerous and varied reasons to engage in option trading. Most involve the desire to make money. Some people use strategies as defenses against incurring losses on stocks they already own. If you own 100 shares of Dell Computers and are afraid of a market correction, you might want to buy a put option as a hedge against possible losses. Owning a put option will give you the right to sell your Dell shares at the specified strike price, regardless of the stock price drop.

Conversely, you have no intention of selling your Dell shares and expect the share price to rise very sharply within the next month. In fact, you wish you had another $8,000.00 with which to buy more shares before the expected rise in share price. The less expensive alternative – Buy a call option. The current Dell share price is $80.00, you learn that one contract of next month's Dell call option, with a strike price of $80.00, would cost you 2 1/4 , or $2.25 per share X 100 shares = $225.00. For $225.00 you could have control over another 100 shares of Dell stock. If the stock price were to rise, you could exercise the option, buy the stock for the lower share price of $80.00 and profit the difference just as if you had owned the stock, but without risking the full price of $8,000.00. If the stock price fell, or stayed the same, your loss would be $225.00. This is active risk management.

There seems to be a very real phenomenon associated with owning stocks. Many people, faced with a loss in their investments, refuse to realize that the loss is possibly due to an even deeper weakness in some factor of the stock's parent company. Instead of divesting themselves of that particular stock, they will doggedly hang on, hoping to regain money that is long-gone. If an underlying stock shows signs of weakness, be prepared to close that position at an advantageous time, and move to a better opportunity. Picking superior stocks for option trading is probably the most difficult aspect of the entire process. Be very selective, do your research and develop a sense of timing. If you find you are not expert in picking stocks suitable for option trading, you are in good and crowded company. Fortunately, there are several subscription advisory services available to option traders, who actively make those difficult choices for you. They employ extremely sophisticated software and research methods to find just the right stocks with the proper profile potential to succeed in option trading.

Whatever brokerage firm you choose to handle your account, be aware that in this era of massive trading volume, brokerage houses have had to accelerate training for their employees. Just because they can efficiently take your order over the phone in no way indicates they understand option trading. In fact, you might know more than they do.

You should either, perform your own research, pick your own stocks, or hire a professional to do it for you. Whichever you choose, track your successes and failures. Do not ask, or expect, your broker to advise you in trading options unless they are hired to offer such advice. Even so, be alert.

Stock trading is pretty simple and straightforward. First you buy the stock, then you wait until, hopefully, the stock rises in price before selling it for a profit. That is a logical predictable order of events. However, option trading is a bit more complex, which probably adds to its mystery. When you ***buy a call***, it is much like buying stock except, ***you purchase a right, instead of the actual stock***. In addition, you only pay a fraction of the stock's actual value to be able to control it, and your limitations are time-related. You wait until the underlying stock price rises, then sell the option for a profit. Buying puts works in a similar manner, except in reverse. You want the stock price to fall, instead of rise, but the order is logical – Buy, then sell. Now, we come to selling calls, and selling puts… different concepts.

Chapter 15: Selling Short

"Selling short"…

To the uninitiated, those two simple words can strike fear in their hearts and cause their minds to slam shut. Let's dissect short-selling to expose the unvarnished truth. We will help you discover an effective way to make money selling short… and with minimum risk.

As previously mentioned, the logical transaction is to buy, then sell. Short-selling is just the reverse, and it's every bit as safe. First we sell, then, we buy. Once you familiarize yourself with the actual mechanics of the strategy it becomes just another way to reach your desired goals. Short selling goes on all around you, and in many forms.

Examples:

The newspaper boy sells you a subscription to his paper. He takes your money then later buys the set amount of papers from his company for delivery to his subscribers.

A housing developer sells houses first, using plans and photos, then, uses that money to finance construction costs to build the houses later.

A grocer orders 10 cases of soup from his wholesaler. He takes delivery and receives a bill for his order, which he has to pay within 30 days. He sells the soup one can at a time. Then pays his bill with the money he earned; selling, then buying.

These examples use **Other-People's-Money (OPM)** to finance profits. There is nothing strange or mysterious about the process. Why shouldn't you do the same thing? It is a normal course of action and the way business is conducted.

If you want to sell a stock option call, or a put, you don't have to buy it first. You simply initiate a *sell* order with your broker to sell one contract of ABC May 27 calls (currently selling for $2.00 per share), with a strike price of 27.

Sell one contract ABC May 27 Call for 2, to open your position.

Your account will be credited with the $200.00 premium you received for selling the option. (100 shares of ABC stock, at $2.00 per share = $200.00). As simple, as that transaction sounds, it is only half-complete. We will finish it later. **Your hope is that the ABC stock price will fall, the option will not be exercised, but expire, worthless. If so, you will capture the entire $200.00 premium as profit**. However, if the stock price rises to ITM by expiration date of the option, you will either be required to furnish 100 shares of ABC stock at the strike price, or pay the difference between the option's strike price and the stock's current share price. **However, as a seller, you have one more option**. While watching price movements of ABC stock you notice an upward trend in price. If the stock reaches a level of several points ITM the option becomes profitable for its owner to exercise, and you want to prevent that occurrence. Therefore, you initiate another order with your broker to *buy back* the option, **and close it, before it has a chance to be exercised**. At that point your option has experienced one complete turnaround. You opened your position with a sell order, then, closed it by buying the option back. Depending upon the timing involved, buying the option back could cost more than you received in premium when you sold it, but it further reduces potential risks, and losses.

WHERE'S THE PROFIT?

Normally, option *sellers* only want their options to expire so they can capture the entire premium as profit. If the underlying stock performs as planned, it will fall in price, and the seller can do just that. If his research is accurate, that is the expected outcome. However, if his research is faulty, inaccurate, incomplete, or just plain wrong, and the stock price rises instead, then he must employ further risk management in order to avoid unexpected, and potentially large, losses.

We sold an ABC call option for 2 ($200.00) when it was OTM (the stock price of $24.00 was below the strike price of $27.00). When the stock price increased to $30.00 per share, a level above the strike price, the option became ITM making it more valuable on the market, and to its owner. In order to prevent the exercise of the option we decide to buy it back. It might be necessary to pay a greater amount than the $200.00 we received. But, we are managing our risks against an even further fall in the stock price. Now that the option is ITM it is selling for 3, or $300.00. Upon closing our position the transaction would end up costing us $100.00, plus brokerage fees. $300.00 (we paid to close the position) - $200.00 (premium we received to open the position) = $100.00 loss. However, relative to purchasing the stock for $3000.00 then furnishing it to the buyer for $2400.00, or having to pay the difference between the stock price of $30.00 and the strike price of $27.00 ($3.00 X 100 shares = $300.00), we managed our risk very well.

Our cost in buying back the option = $100.00. Our cost with option exercised = $300.00.

While this scenario does occasionally happen, it is hopefully not a common occurrence. During our research for stocks to use in option trading we would normally select better candidates. The above example was shown to highlight possibilities, and does not necessarily portend probabilities. Having exposed one of the less attractive aspects of selling options, consider this: Hopefully, the stocks we pick will perform as expected, after all, that is why they were selected in the first place. ***Most options we <u>sell</u> will be closed in one of three ways:***

- They will expire, allowing us to capture the entire premium as profit.
- We will buy the option back, closing the position before expiration, normally realizing a sure profit. However, in the event of an unexpected movement of the underlying stock, it is possible that the option must be repurchased before expiration to prevent a possible loss.
- The third possible way a sold option can be closed is by exercise. While this action can be beneficial to us under certain circumstances, we generally take action to avoid the occurrence.

Summary:

When we sell an option prior to first buying it, we assume a ***short*** position. A complete turnaround occurs when we buy back the same option, closing the position. An alternative is to allow it to expire, creating self-cancellation. In most cases we can afford to wait until the stock's movement is advantageous to us. As sellers… time is on our side.

Remember:

- As a *call buyer*, our potential risk is limited to the premium we paid for the option.
- As a *call seller*, our risk is unlimited, and should <u>always</u> be offset with the purchase of a similar call.

When we *sell* options we want them to expire so we can capture the entire premium paid to us as profit. But we know that there is unlimited risk in selling options, so it doesn't seem prudent to engage in that form of option trading. Consider this – Suppose there was a way to reduce that very real, unlimited risk associated with selling options contracts, leaving strong upside potential. When we *purchase* a stock option we are indicating that we possibly want to either buy, or sell, that stock, and are willing to pay a premium to freeze the purchase price until a specified time in the future. By that predetermined date we will make that final decision based upon the value of the stock at that time. If the value of the stock, moves in our favor we will exercise the option, and buy, or sell, the stock at the previously agreed upon price. If the value of the stock does not move in our favor, we will allow the option to expire, and will forfeit the premium we paid for it.

In contrast, if we were to purchase the same amount of stock outright, and the share price dropped significantly (Which sometimes happens), then we could suffer serious losses. Owning options, on the other hand, allows us to purchase the stock only if it has already increased in value, creating a meaningful hedge against risk. The premium we pay for the privilege of owning that hedge is minimal. By controlling the disposition of the option, the outcome of our investment is greatly tilted in our favor. While we don't have control over which way the stock price will move, we do have control over what to do with the stock once it has moved. We only participate if the stock price moves in a direction profitable to us.

These options are simply not available to us in stock and mutual fund ownership. If our fund value rises, we make money – if it falls, we lose money. We have two choices, stay in for all the ups and downs of market swings, or get out. Optimum risk management in stocks and mutual funds is simply not an option.

Some time ago I had an unpleasant conversation with my then mutual fund supervisor. I was absolutely certain that the market was due for a serious correction. I wanted to temporarily move my invested money into their money market fund... within the same fund family. Then, after the market had bottomed out, I had intended to repurchase my old funds. There were thousands of dollars at risk. My fund representative did not like the idea at all. He was blatantly insensitive to the very real likelihood of my impending losses due to remaining invested in my original funds. Company management had set an arbitrary, yearly limit of four switches, even within their own funds, and no amount of logic would sway the company's thinking. They wanted total and absolute control over my investments and were not interested in allowing me to manage my own risks against certain losses. The market correction did occur, and I saved thousands of dollars by avoiding that major market drop then riding it up again. I also found another mutual fund that allowed me to actively manage my own risks. Mutual funds are wonderful financial vehicles. But, they do have serious limitations in maximizing investor's profits.

One more piece of information concerning mutual funds: Occasionally, very popular and successful mutual funds close their doors to new investors. The stated reason for this "Lock-out" is that the closure is in the best interest of its investors by keeping the fund at an optimum size, and with less money to deal with, or manage, they are able to keep the fund more profitable. This explanation is partially true most of the time. But watch closely the next time your mutual fund closes to new investors. Fund analysts are well aware of cyclical trends within their holdings. For example, a large cap fund has been riding a high earnings wave, and their analysts believe large cap stocks will soon fall into disfavor. They will close the fund to new investors in order to discourage their current investors from vacating the fund, and racing toward the newest hot sector. After a fund has been closed, you are not allowed to re-enter it until the fund reopens, which could be years in the future. A tactic used to retain the fund's investments, but may not be in the best interest of the investor.

After you have learned how options respond to market conditions, and what actions are available to you in order to capitalize on those events, using our strategy becomes a simple matter of routine.

Section 2: The Real World of Option Trading

Chapter 16: An Ideal Scenario

The following examples outline events in a near-perfect scenario:

We have completed extensive research on ABC stock and are **ready to try a put option spread**. Our first step is to purchase a long-term put option with an expiration date six months in the future. The long-term puts we buy are used exclusively as a continuous hedge against selling opposing, short-term puts. Occasionally, both the long-term puts and the short-term puts will have the same strike price, but the expiration dates will differ.

Date: February 3rd. The ABC stock price is $20.00 per share.

We ***buy*** 1 contract ABC July 20 Put for 4 (Long term). We simultaneously ***sell*** 1 contract ABC February 20 Put for 1 (Short term). Only three weeks remain before the February expiration date arrives. The option has little time-value remaining.

Reiterating, the **only** reason we ***buy*** **long-term puts is as a hedge against our short-term put position. They have no other value**. The reason will soon become clear. We then ***sell*** **a short-term put on the same stock, and with the same strike price, but with different expiration dates**. Our aim is for the ABC stock price to rise, making the option that we ***sold***, worthless to its owner. We paid 4, or $400.00, for the long, July option we ***bought***, and simultaneously received a $100.00 premium for the short, February 20 put we ***sold***. In order for the short, February 20 option to lose its value and expire, it would be necessary for the ABC stock price to rise above the strike price, to more than $20.00 per share by expiration.

The stock price indeed rose to $22.00 per share at expiration. The option was allowed to expire, allowing us to capture the entire $100.00 premium as profit.

Date: February 21, Options Expiration Day (OED).

The short, Feb 20 put expires, OTM. We capture the entire $100.00 premium, and are now free to sell another short-term put, while keeping the July, long-term put in force.

We previously **bought** a July 20 put for 4 = $400.00 debit. We **sold** the Feb 20 put for 1 = $100.00 credit.

$400.00 debit - $100.00 credit = $300.00 initial spread **debit**. Our cost basis for the option spread has now been reduced from a $400.00, to a $300.00 **debit**.

We **sell** 1 contract ABC March 20 Put for 2 1/2, and received a $250.00 premium. In the meantime, the ABC stock price fluctuates between $19.00 and $22.00 per share. With the arrival of March expiration day, the ABC stock price is $21.00. Our March option expires, allowing us to capture the entire $250.00 premium as profit.

The adjusted spread debit of our option is $300.00 - $250.00 premium credit received = $50.00 adjusted spread **debit**. At this interval, the cost basis for our option spreads has been significantly and systematically reduced.

At March expiration we sell an April 20 Put for 2, or $200.00, then watch the movement of the stock. When April expiration date arrives, the ABC stock price has spiked up to $24.00 per share. Again, the option expires, allowing us to profit the $200.00 premium. Premium captured is $200.00 - $50.00 adjusted spread **debit** = $150.00 adjusted spread **credit**. As you can plainly see, the cost of our evolving option spread has been reduced from $300.00 initial **debit**, to a **credit** of $150.00, and we still have three months to capture more premiums. We do not make money from the rise and fall of the underlying stock price, in the conventional sense, but in capturing premiums from expired, short-term options bought by speculators. In doing this, we assume the position of the "House", as time is working against the speculators, while being firmly on our side. The long July Put we purchased has acted as a continuous hedge, or an insurance policy, against the risk of the possibility of the ABC stock sharply falling, creating a situation whereby the option's owner could exercise it at a potential loss for us.

If we did not own an opposing, long Put option as a hedge against the short Put options we sold, we would be "Uncovered", and exposed to unlimited risk. With each put option we sell, with a strike price of 20, the buyer has the right to exercise that option and sell us 100 shares of ABC stock for $20.00 per share. If the ABC stock had dropped to $15.00 per share and our short option were exercised by its owner, we would be forced to buy 100 shares of ABC stock for $20.00 per share. However, by owning the opposing long Put, we would simply exercise it, allowing us to sell the same 100 shares of ABC stock for the same $20.00 per share. Therefore, we incurred no loss except for trading fees. Our insurance policy worked. For the premium we paid for our long July option, we have hedge insurance continuously in force for the six-month lifetime of our spreads, or until the option is exercised. We have effectively managed our risks.

As each short Put option expires, we continue to sell another one each month, capturing profits on their expirations. Our long July 20 Put expires on the 3rd Saturday of that month. On June's expiration day, if we want to sell the last remaining option against our long July option, we must make a small change. In *selling* a *short* July 20 Put option against our *long* July 20 Put option, both options effectively cancel each other out. To close a *short* May 50 Call, you simply *purchase* a May 50 Call. To close a long July 20 Put, you sell a short July 20 Put. That action creates a complete turnaround by buying, and then selling, the same option. On June expiration day there is still one more monthly premium to be captured before our hedge protection runs out on the long July 20 Put option. In June, the ABC stock price was $27.00. In order to avoid self-cancellation, we sell a short ABC July 25 Put against our long July 20 Put position. This maneuver allows us to keep both options in force while also changing the basic fundamentals and risks involved. Remember the parallel twins, risk and reward? We are about to see them at work once again.

In checking option prices on the CBOE web site, we discover that the ABC July 25 Put option is worth considerably more than the ABC July 20 Puts we had previously been selling. The July 20 Put option is selling for only $1.00, while the July 25 Put option is selling for 3. Since both options are OTM, neither have intrinsic value, only time value remains. The principle reason the July 25 Put is worth more is due to its strike price being closer to the actual stock price. The amount of time remaining until expiration makes the July 25 Put (only 2 points away) easier to reach ITM status than the July 20 Put (7 points away). Therefore, the July 25 Put is more valuable. When the strike prices of both our long and short puts were the same, we were completely hedged against potential losses from a sudden fall in price of the underlying stock. However, by creating a spread-gap of 5 points between the strike prices of our two options, we have created a greater risk factor, along with a higher profit potential.

Consider this: We are long a July 20 Put, and short a July 25 Put. Let's suppose the ABC stock price plunges to $15.00 per share. The short July 25 Put is exercised, and we are obligated to buy 100 shares of ABC stock for $25.00 per share. Our long July 20 Put, when exercised, allows us to sell the same 100 shares of ABC stock, but at the strike price of $20.00 per share. In having a disparity between the two options' strike prices we are at risk of a potential loss of $5.00 per share, or $500.00. The strike price of our long July 20 Put is set, and cannot be moved, unless we choose to close the position and purchase another one with the strike price closer to the actual price of the stock. We do have the choice of selling a put option with its strike price closer to the actual stock price, making the option more valuable. But in taking that action, we also add more risk by widening the strike price gap within the spread. We must be willing to accept the parallel risk vs. reward within the spread.

A word about *margin*: In the above example of owning a long July 20 Put, and selling a short July 25 Put, we have a 5 point inherent risk, or $500.00 in the option spread. If the option was exercised, and we could not cover the loss, our broker could be liable for it. Therefore, at the initial activation of the option spread we will be required to post a bond, of sorts, for that $500.00 risk. Our brokerage will set aside that amount from our account, and deposit it into our "Margin" account. If the option is not exercised, then we will be re-credited with the $500.00. If the option is exercised, the $500.00 margin will be used to make up the difference between the two strike prices and cover our debt caused by the exercise. The margin system protects both the trader, as well as the brokerage, and promotes a smooth trading system.

Chapter 17: Trading With an Advisory Service

Let's do another complete turnaround. Our computer is in the shop for repair, and we find we don't have the time or means to complete the necessary research on a potential stock option candidate. Instead, we decide to hire a professional to help us pick an appropriate stock, plus offer sound trading and timing advice. We are advised to initiate the following put option spread:

Date – January 2nd XYZ stock price is $50.00 per share.

Buy one contract XYZ May 50 Put for 3, and simultaneously,

Sell one contract XYZ Jan 50 Put for 1 1/2.

- **January expiration day**:

XYZ stock price is $51.50 per share.

The January option expires and we capture the $150.00 premium as profit.

$300.00 paid for the long Put - $150.00 received for the short, January Put = $150.00 initial spread debit.

We sell an XYZ February 50 Put for 2 ¼ .

- **February Expiration day**:

XYZ stock price is $55.00 per share.

The February option expires, and we keep the premium of $225.00 - $150.00, the initial spread

Debit = $75.00 adjusted net credit.

With the expiration of this option we have totally paid for our insurance, the long May 50 Put option, and are earning substantial profits on our spreads.

We sell an XYZ March 50 Put spread for 2.

- **March Expiration day**:

XYZ stock price is $57.50.

The March option expires, and we keep the premium of $200.00 + the previous credit of $75.00 = $275.00 adjusted net credit.

The XYZ April 50 Puts are suddenly, selling very cheaply at 7/8. Our advisory service informs us that due to an internal problem within the XYZ company, activity in XYZ stock trading has slowed but, the company is still sound. We decide that the premium of 7/8 of a point is not worth the trouble in selling the April 50 Puts. The XYZ stock price is now $57.00. We decide to sell an XYZ April 55 Put for 4, instead. This new strike price causes us to incur more risk, but the greater premium value seems worth it. (Due to the 5 point strike price disparity between our long and short positions, our margin account will be assessed $500.00 pending the outcome of the option's disposition.)

- **April Expiration day**:

XYZ stock price is $58.00.

Our April option expires, and we capture the $400.00 premium as profit.

$400.00 + $275.00 = $ 675.00 adjusted net credit.

We sell an XYZ May 55 Put for 3.

- **May expiration day** is on May 20th.

On May 8, we are informed by our advisory service that the XYZ stock price will likely fall soon, due to lower than expected company revenues. They advise us to buy back the May 55 Put option for 2, or $200.00, closing the position. We followed their advice and,

Bought XYZ May 55 Put for 2.

This action prevented our May 55 Put option from being exercised. The XYZ stock soon fell to $45.00 per share moving our short May 55 Put option to ITM. If the option had been exercised, we would have incurred a loss of $500.00, the difference between our two option's strike prices. In buying the option back for $200.00, we still earned $100.00 on the May spread.

$300.00 premium received - $200.00 cost to buy back the option = $100.00 profit.

$100.00 profit + $675.00 previous credit = $775.00 adjusted net credit.

It is worth noting that had we waited until after the XYZ stock price decrease, and even before the option could be exercised by its owner, it would have been increasingly more expensive to withdraw from the position. As the stock price dropped from $57.00 to $45.00 the option moved more and more to a position of ITM. As this occurred, the price of the option also increased in value and could have cost us dearly to buy it back. When the stock price finally bottomed out at $45.00 per share, the price of the option had increased to $1100.00. Thankfully, we were able to close our position while the option was still OTM, and relatively inexpensive. Having both our long and short options in force, our total risk exposure was $500.00. We managed our risk well.

An added benefit:

We did buy back and close our short May 55 Put, but let's not forget about our long May 50 Put, which we still own. When the XYZ stock price bottomed at $45.00 per share, that moved our long May 50 option to ITM status by 5 points. We have the right to sell 100 shares of XYZ stock for our strike price of $50.00 per share. If we do not want to sell the actual shares, we can choose to be credited with the difference between our option's strike price, and the current stock price. We can now sell a May 50 Put to close that position for a profit of 5 ½, or $550.00. (For every point an option is ITM, plus ½ point of time value remaining.)

Intrinsic value of the option, $500.00 + $50.00 time value remaining = $550.00 + previous profit of $750.00 = $1250.00 net profit.

We mentioned previously that the long puts we purchase have no other purpose than to act as a hedge for the short puts we sell. Occasionally, when conditions are favorable, we get an added bonus. Timing allowed us to capitalize further on the long puts we owned.

In the previous examples we have shown you how to make money using our put option strategies in a near-perfect world scenario. The following is a more probable, realistic view.

As you saw in our "Perfect World" scenario, nearly all of our expectations were predictably met. All except one of our short positions expired, allowing us to keep the entire premium as profit. After all possible short puts had been sold against our long put-hedge, we were even able to sell our long put for a handsome profit. That much good fortune is possibly a bit more than we can routinely expect on a day-to-day basis. Therefore, we will now add a few glitches to the normal ups and downs of the stock market, while showing you how to further manage the associated risks.

Chapter 18: Welcome to the Real World

A friend recommended PEW, a perfume stock, as a possible candidate for option trading. We know his testimonial isn't really the best way to choose an underlying stock. But, we try it anyway.

Date: April 2nd PEW stock is selling for $30.00 per share. We:

Buy one contract PEW Aug 30 Puts for 3 ½ $350.00

Sell one contract PEW April 30 Puts for 1 $100.00

$350.00 - $100.00 = $250.00 initial spread debit.

At expiration day the stock price has risen to $36.00 per share. The April 30 Put expires OTM for its owner and, we keep the $100.00 premium. We check option prices on the CBOE web site and learn that PEW May 30 Put options are selling for ½ (0.50). The price doesn't seem worthwhile to us, so we decide to:

Sell one contract PEW May 35 Puts for 2 ($200.00)

During May, the PEW stock price fluctuates, then, falls to $25.00 per share by expiration day. Our long put has a strike price of 30, while our short put has a strike price of 35. The 5-point difference between the two strike prices indicates that we have a risk exposure of $500.00. If the underlying stock price were to rise, we wouldn't be at risk. (Example: If it were to fall to $10.00 per share, our risk would still be limited to the difference between the strike prices, 5 points = $500.00 on our spread position.)

As the PEW stock price fell to $25.00 per share, our short option was exercised, obligating us to buy 100 shares of PEW stock at $35.00 per share. In order for us to recover from the exercise of the option, we must also exercise our long put option and sell the same 100 shares of PEW stock at the long option's strike price of $30.00 per share, suffering a $500.00 loss.

That $500.00 loss added to our remaining spread option purchase debit of $250.00 = $750.00 net adjusted spread debit. You can easily see that options can also be very risky. There are at least two different ways we could have managed the risks involved in our option spread.

Hindsight tells us that perhaps we should have picked better, more stable, less risky stocks upon which to base our options.

By acting before the stock price fell. (requiring timely knowledge of the stock's impending plunge from research, news media, or an advisory service.) Even after the stock price began to fall, we could have limited our loss by buying back our short position when the stock price was anywhere between $30.00 and $25.00 per share.

The best way to succeed with any investment is to systematically manage known risks down to the lowest possible level, and to eliminate any "Pop-up" risks as quickly as possible. It is imperative to know and understand, ahead of time, exactly what actions to take at the time those risks materialize. Outcomes, such as the one depicted above, do sometimes occur. Even with the best possible research available, re-figuring and plotting every known pitfall will not prevent stock prices from moving contrary to our predictions…and for no apparent reason. You will occasionally lose money by trading options. Understand, accept, and prepare yourself for that eventuality. By practicing the proven risk management techniques contained in this book, you can learn to lessen those losses. We decide to abandon the PEW stock as a viable candidate for option trading.

Our option-trading advisor recommends XXX as an underlying stock suitable for options trading. We do some preliminary research on our own and decide to take the advice.

Date: Feb 2nd XXX stock price is $31.00.

Our option advisory service recommends we:

Buy 5 contracts XXX July 30 Puts for 5 ($2500.00)

Sell 5 contracts XXX Feb 30 Puts for 2 ¼ ($1125.00). This option is OTM.

February Expiration day, XXX stock price is $36.00 per share. The option expires OTM, allowing us to capture the $1125.00 as profit. $2500.00 - $1125.00 = $1375.00 initial spread debit.

We then:

Sell XXX March 35 Puts for 3 ½ ($1750.00)

One week before March expiration the XXX stock price rises to $39.00. Simultaneously, our short March 35 Put option has decayed to a value of 1/16 of a point ($31.25)

Strategy: The March 35 Put now has a value of 1/16 of a point remaining. If we act now, we can buy back the option and simultaneously sell an April 35 Put option for 2 7/8. If we wait until the March 35 Put expires, we could capture an extra 1/16 of a point of profit vs. buying the option back early. However, also at expiration, the value of the April 35 Put option will have decayed to 2 ¼, a loss of 5/8 of a point in the potential premium we could receive for the early sale.

We decide to buy back the March 35 Put option for 1/16, and simultaneously sell the April 35 Put option for 2 7/8. In buying back the option early, the 1/16 of a point costs us $31.25 in previously received premiums. In selling the April 35 Put option at 2 7/8 vs. 2 ¼ , we were able to gain 5/8 (0.625) of a point of premium, or 0.625 x 500 shares = $312.50. $312.50 - $31.25 = $281.25 profits, over those we could have realized at expiration. (This strategy not only maximizes profits, but also maximizes risk management.)

Our adjusted net spread debit, $3175.00 + $31.25 buy back price = $1406.25 new adjusted spread Debit. We: Bought-back XXX March 35 Puts for 1/16 ($31.25) and

Sold XXX April 35 Puts for 2 7/8 ($1437.50).

Adjusted spread debit $1406.25 - $1437.50 premium received = $31.25 new adjusted spread Credit.

April 15, one week before expiration, and a similar situation to the March scenario, the XXX stock price has risen to $40.00 per share. Our April 35 Put option is still OTM, and its time value has decayed to 1/8 of a point, or $62.50. We look at the CBOE exchange option listings, and discover that the XXX May 40 Puts are selling for 3 ¼ . If we wait until after expiration, the May 40 Puts will likely decay to around the 2 7/8 range. If we act now, we can buy back the April 35 Puts at

1/8 of a point ($62.50), and simultaneously sell the May 40 Puts for 3 ¼ ($1625.00). We will realize an extra ¼ point of premium vs. allowing the April 35 Puts to expire, then selling the May 40 Puts a week from now, for 2 7/8.

The difference between 3 ¼ , the current price of the May 40 Puts, and the 2 7/8, the expected price of the May 40 Puts after expiration, is 3/8 of a point. Then, subtract the cost of buying back the option, 1/8 of a point, and we have net savings of ¼ point. We:

Buy back the April 35 Puts for 1/8 or 0.125 x 500 shares = $62.50.

Adjusted spread credit $31.25 - $62.50 cost of buyback = $31.25 new adjusted spread debit.

Sell the May 40 Puts for 3 ¼ , or 3.25 x 500 shares = $1625.00.

$1625.00 premium received - $31.25 adjusted spread debit = $1,593.75 new adjusted spread credit.

On May 10th, the XXX stock price falls to $37.50. We suspect that a further drop in price might be in store, so we buy-back our XXX May 40 Put option before the stock price falls below our protective hedge rand of $30.00. Because the XXX stock price is already below our May option strike price of $40.00, the value of the option is increasing exponentially with every point drop in the stock price, along with the cost of our intended buyback. The XXX May 40 option is now ITM. We: Buy back the XXX May 40 Put option for 3 ½ ($1750.00).

Strategy: If we had known that the XXX stock price would not have fallen any further than $37.00 per share, we could have held the May 40 option until the owner chose to exercise it. Our losses would have been limited to 3, or 3 x 500 shares = $1500.00. **That information was not available to us**. Therefore, we managed our risk based on the *possibility* that the XXX stock price could decline even further. If the XXX stock price had fallen below $30.00 per share, our maximum hedge exposure would have been 10, or 10 x 500 shares = $5,000.00. We effectively managed our risk by buying back the ITM, May 40 Put option.

We did not sell a succeeding XXX June Put at that time, choosing to wait until the XXX stock price stabilized. When it bottomed at $34.00 per share, we sold XXX June 35 Put options for 4, after consultation with our advisory service. Research indicated the stock would rise to its former levels within 2 to 3 weeks. Normally, we would not sell ITM Put options, (XXX stock price was $34.00 per share, and our June Puts had a strike price of $35.00) rendering the June 35 Put options ITM by 1, or 1 x 500 shares = $500.00. We will watch the XXX stock very closely, and if it were to show signs of sliding downward, we would be ready to take appropriate action.

Summary of transaction: We:

Bought back XXX May 40 Puts for 3 ½ ($1750.00) and

Sold XXX June 35 Puts for 4 ($2,000.00).

Adjusted spread credit $1718.75 - $1750.00 buy-back of May 40 Puts = $31.25 adjusted spread debit. $31.25 debit + $2,000.00 premium received for June 35 Puts = $1968.75 adjusted spread credit.

The XXX stock price did rise to $38.00 by the middle of June. Our advisor suggested we:

Buy back XXX June 35 Puts for 3/16 of a point ($93.75) and simultaneously

Sell XXX July 35 Puts for 3 3/8 ($1,687.50). We followed their advice.

Adjusted spread credit $1968.75 - $93.75 buyback of June 35 Puts = $1875.00 adjusted spread credit. $1875.00 + $1687.50 premium received for July 35 Puts = $3562.50 new adjusted spread credit.

The XXX stock price remained above $38.00 through July. Since our long July 30 Put option expired in July, we simply allowed our short July 35 options to expire at the same time. However, a further strategy would be to periodically check the prices of both our long July 30 Put option, as well as our short July 35 option. It is quite possible to take full advantage of both decaying option prices before expiration, and simultaneously:

Buy back short XXX July 35 Puts and Sell our long July 30 Puts to earn an extra profit over waiting for expiration.

This action would nail down profits and remove them from further risk. It would also free-up invested capital, as well as margin requirement funds, allowing the profits to be further invested. Let's look at our profile:

The initial, long July 30 Puts we purchased cost us $2,500.00.

At the same time, we received $1,125.00 for the Feb 30 Puts we sold. Our initial spread debit was $1,375.00. Our ending spread credit was $3,562.50.

$3,562.50 ending spread credit - $1,375.00 initial spread debit = $2,187.50 profit on the entire life of the spread, or 159%.

Throughout the life of the option spread we managed our risks well, while using several strategies to continually maximize our profits. Even though we may not use all the strategies available to us, we need to at least consider, and evaluate them relative to the constantly changing values of our options. For optimum results learn to work out each scenario in advance, deciding each action to take as the particulars of the option changes. In taking the time and effort to thoroughly learn these strategies, along with the necessary calculations, you will likely find the process becoming repetitive and second nature to you. Put forth the effort now and enjoy the confidence that comes from knowing you are using your own abilities to maximize profits, while also effectively managing risks.

The following position would be considered in the volatile category. It is an actual recommendation and trade that was made and experienced. While not an everyday occurrence, perhaps, similar results as these are frequently reported.

On April 1st, 1998, while INTU stock was selling for $50.50 per share, our advisor recommended their clients buy Call options with the long-term expiration date of January 1999, and at a strike price of $60.00 per share. At the same time, they also recommended their clients write (sell) short-term Call options on the same stock expiring in June, and with a strike price of 60.

The above transaction occurred simultaneously, with the following result:

Cost of purchase was 4.25 – 2.125 premium received = a net spread debit of 2.125 per share.

On the 3rd Friday in June the Call option written (sold) in April, expired, while the stock reached a share value of $56.50, way short of the strike price of 60.

We then sold (wrote) another INTU Call option with the same strike price of 60, but this time expiring in August, and received a premium of 3.375 per share x 100 shares = $337.50. The sale moved us into credit territory because the combined revenue received from both sold options was 3.375 + 2.125 = 5.50. Subtract the cost of the original long hedge-option previously purchased,

5.50 – 4.25 = 1.25 credit.

Purchase cost, long-term hedge option = 4.25.

Premium earned on first option sale = 2.125.

Premium earned on second option sale = 3.375.

The client is now in positive territory with a net credit of 1.25 per share. In August, the sold option was again allowed to expire because the stock had dropped to 44.625 per share.

We sold another Call option, this time for November and at a strike price of 60, which resulted in a premium of 1.50. That option also expired, as the stock price in November was 58.75. Profit so far... almost 130%. The Client held on to the Jan 20 Call option and eventually sold it for 38, when the stock was trading at 98. (Strike price of 60, with increase in stock price to 98... 98 – 60 = 38 x 100 shares = $3800.00.) For every dollar the stock price rises above ITM, the option value increases exponentially.

Chapter 19: Margin – How Does It Really Work?

The use of margin in option trading is simply another form of risk management. Your broker will impose margin requirements onto your option account both for reasons of managing his own risk against possible losses, which could be incurred within your trading portfolio, and for your own protection. A ***margin account*** is simply money set aside to ensure adequate coverage of option positions that could be in jeopardy in the event of option exercise. It also serves as a holding account from which brokerage fees, as well as the costs you will incur in buying option contracts, are routinely withdrawn. Because you must furnish 100% of the money required for margins, there is no need to borrow to satisfy the requirement. **There are three routine events that normally trigger money being withdrawn from your margin account.** **Two of the three,** *trading fees* **and** *costs of options you purchase*, **are actually charges, and will not be refunded. The third, and by far the largest of the three,** *is to cover built-in risk factors between strike-price value differences within your opposing option positions*. **Upon closing an option with a built-in risk factor, these funds are returned to your margin account, as the associated risk is no longer present.** *Margin* **could be seen merely as a risk-managed emergency and general fund.**

At the beginning of every trade day ask your broker for your *"Free cash"* and *"Margin"* positions. **Your *"Free cash"* is the amount of money you have available to buy options. Your *"Margin"* is the total amount being held to back-up any associated risks due to specific, open positions within your account.** We have included a margin-tracking column within the Profitability Trade Log spreadsheet. It allows you to keep track of all your option requirements as they occur, as well as when they no longer apply to your positions.

In buying stocks outright, you purchase a tangible asset. If you were to purchase those stocks using a margin account, you would only be required to put up half the purchase price. Your brokerage firm would lend you the other half. The broker then uses the stock as collateral for the loan. This arrangement makes it possible to buy more shares than would be possible otherwise. Also, the brokerage firm earns interest on the loan it makes to you. Interest rates vary from broker to broker. Stocks are generally considered to have a **"Base"** value, which is usually below their normal trading range. It is the actual, intrinsic value of the company's tangible assets. Therefore, brokerages can afford to lend you money in the form of margin, based on that intrinsic value. If the share price of the stock you purchased increases, your broker will allow you to borrow additional sums. But if the stock share-price were to fall beyond an acceptable value, normally 30% to 35% of the value of the security, you would receive a "**Margin Call**" from your broker, asking for more money. The margin call directs you to deposit more money into your margin account to make up for the loss in value of your stock. You normally have three days to comply. If you cannot provide the necessary funds to cover the margin call, the broker has the right to sell your existing positions at a potentially serious loss to you. The situation forces you to turn a possible, unrealized loss into a realized one. You have the obligation to supply them with either the security, or the money you owe.

Your brokerage firm can freely adjust your cash and margin accounts to cover normal fees and charges incurred in trading; also, to compensate for any adverse strike-price imbalances due to uncovered risks. The fees and charges include:

- **Cost of the option**. This is the price you pay for the option, i.e.,

When you purchase an ABC May 40 Put for 2, the cost of the option is $2.00 per share. For one contract the price would be $200.00. You are required to have this amount available in your cash or margin account at the time of the trade.

- **Funds equaling any uncovered exposure between the strike prices of the options you are selling, and the ones you own, i.e.,**

Long one contract ABC May 40 Put, and short one contract ABC April 45 Put. The margin requirement here is 5, or $500.00.

- **Brokerage fees levied against your account for each option transaction made.**

There is one more possible charge that could be added to the three listed above:

- **The naked position requirement**.

Since **we do <u>not</u> advocate you <u>ever</u> being in an exposed (naked) position**, the naked requirements will not be covered here. However, a brief explanation follows.

<u>NAKED</u>.

<u>Initial Regulation T requirements</u>:

<u>Example</u>:

You sell an ABC May 50 Put for 2, with no opposing hedge against your position. You are exposed… naked. The buyer of that option has the right to sell 100 shares of ABC stock to you for $50.00 per share, no matter how low the stock price may plunge. You virtually have unlimited risk down to the base value of the stock in this position, because you are not "**Covered**" by an opposing option purchase, nor do you presently own 100 shares of ABC stock. Normally, a broker should not allow you to become "**Uncovered**", or "**Naked**" in a position. Therefore the following calculations are used only in spread positions. It is possible to borrow money from your margin account for use in option trading, but the risks are very high, the requirements very complicated, and therefore should be considered by only the most knowledgeable traders. **<u>We do not advocate engaging in the practice.</u>**

All calculations below assume that you have a minimum of $2,000.00 deposited in your brokerage account, and that you have no outstanding indebtedness with the brokerage. Also, that you are not currently, and will not become, exposed to uncovered, or naked, positions.

<u>Margins For Spreads</u>.

A *"spread"* is a long option position and a short option position within the same type of option. An example would be a position containing both a long call and short call on the same underlying stock. The strike prices may differ, but the options making up the spread must have the same number of underlying shares of the same stock.

Also, the long position cannot have an expiration date that is
- *Earlier* than that of the short option.

For margin purposes, only two kinds of spreads exist:
- **the Call spread,** and
- **the Put spread**.

Example:

Put spread Long Short Margin

ABC May 40 Put for 2 ABC May 45 Put for 1 5

Call Spread – Long Short 0

ABC May 40 Call for 2 ABC Feb 45 Call for 1

Spread transactions are categorized in one of two possible ways:

- Either *margin*, or
- *credit*

and, may be transacted <u>only</u> for ***spread requirement purposes*** within the margin account. The resulting long and short options are subject to separate requirements. The spread margin requirement, explained next, cannot be applied to option positions in *cash* accounts.

Initial and Maintenance Spread Requirements

Call spread requirements (Trading fees differ greatly, and will not be addressed here.)

When an account position is: long a Call, and short a Call, on a specific security, and the long Call does not expire before the short Call, the initial and maintenance margin required is the amount, if any, by which the exercise price of the long call exceeds the exercise price of the short call.

<u>Read that again</u>, then, see the examples below.

Long ABC Oct 25 Call Short ABC Sept 20 Call Margin 5

Long ABC Mar 30 Call Short ABC Feb 35 Call Margin 0

When a position is long a Put, and short a put, on a specific security, and the long Put does not expire before the short Put, the initial and maintenance margin required is the amount, if any, by which the exercise price of the short Put exceeds the exercise price of the long Put.

Long XYZ July 50 Put Short XYZ June 60 Put Margin 10

Long XYZ Sept 60 Put Short XYZ July 60 Put Margin 0

All options will eventually experience a complete turnaround; meaning there will be a purchase, and sale, of the same option, but not necessarily in that order. Therefore, let's briefly review the initial margin required when making an option purchase, as well as the margin released when selling an option.

The initial **Regulation T** margin requirement is for the account holder to have on deposit 100% of the costs of all options purchased in both opening and closing transactions. (When purchasing an option, all costs relating to that purchase must already be on deposit within the cash, or margin, account.)

Conversely, all option *sales*, both opening and closing transactions, will result in the release of 100% of the option sales proceeds into the margin accounts. A closing sale transaction is the sale of an established, previously opened position. An opening sale transaction is the sale that creates a short option position. The amount of funds released when selling an option is first applied to other margin commitments made on the same day as the sales, or (Same-day substitution). After satisfying all of that day's commitments, any remaining margin-release funds are then applied to outstanding Regulation T calls. Finally, any margin release remaining, after these obligations are satisfied, is credited back into the margin account. Any margin funds released by the sale and closure of an open long position, is first applied to any other maintenance requirement indebtedness incurred on the same day. This includes option purchase costs, as well as trading fees levied by your broker. Any remaining funds will be deposited into your margin account. In short, your brokerage will charge your margin account for fees, costs, and risk requirements. The, when the risk is no longer present, they will deposit the risk requirement funds back into your account as a credit.

Determining The Requirement.

The initial and maintenance margin required, whether on a call spread (A long call and a short call), or on a put spread (A long put and a short put), is based on the risk assumed, if any, by the difference in strike prices within the option spread. In taking steps to arrive at the correct margin requirement to be used, we must:

Match the expiration dates of the long and short options. The long option must expire on or after the expiration date of the short option.

Determine the difference in strike prices. In the case of a ***Call spread***, it is the amount, if any, by which the exercise price of the ***long*** Call exceeds the exercise price of the ***short*** Call. In the case of a ***Put spread***, it is the amount, if any, by which the exercise price of the ***short*** Put exceeds the exercise price of the ***long*** Put.

Within the examples used in this chapter, the transactions are made in established margin accounts, and the long options will always expire on or after the expiration date of the short options.

Purchase and sale of Puts on the Same Day.

Please take the time to understand the calculations below, as they represent the very essence in determining margin requirements for option trading.

Puts One Contract:

Long July 50 Put for 2 Short May 45 Put for 3

No margin required, due to short strike price being smaller than long strike price (Puts only). The option was traded for a credit of $1.00 per share.

Sale of short Put = $3.00 per share credit.

Purchase of long Put = $2.00 per share debit.

$3.00 credit - $2.00 debit = $1.00 per share net credit on the spread option trade.

Long July 50 Puts for 2 Short May 55 Puts for 1.
Because the strike price of the short put is **greater** than the strike price of the long put by 5, the margin requirement is 5 x 100 shares = $500.00, plus the purchase of the long position was 2, and the sale of the short option was 1.

2 debit – 1 credit = 1 debit, or $100.00.

$500.00 risk difference in strike prices + $100.00 net option cost = $600.00 total margin requirement.

Long July 50 Put for 2 short May 50 Put for 1.

No normal margin required, due to strike prices being the same.

The purchase of the long option was 2, & the sale of the short option was 1.

2 debit – 1 credit = 1 debit, or $100.00.

$1.00 x 100 shares net option costs.

Purchase and sale of Calls on the Same Day.

Calls One Contract

Long July 50 Call for 2 Short May 45 Call for 1.

Because the strike price of the short Call is **less** than the strike price of the long Call by 5, the margin requirement is 5 x 100 shares = $500.00, plus the purchase of the long option was 2, and the sale of the short option was 1.

2 debit – 1 credit = 1 debit = $100.00 net option costs.

$500.00 risk difference in strike prices + $100.00 Net option cost = $600.00 Total margin requirement.

Long July 50 Call for 2 Short May 55 Call for 1.

No margin requirement, due to strike price of the short option being more than the strike price of the long option (Calls only). The sale of the short option was 1, and the purchase price of the long option was 2.

2 debit – 1 credit = 1 debit.

$1.00 x 100 shares = $100.00 net option costs.

Long July 50 Call for 4 Short May 50 Call for 3.

No margin requirement, due to strike prices being the same. The purchase of the long option was 4, and the sale of the short option was 3.

4 debit – 3 credit = 1 debit.

$1.00 x 100 shares = $100.00 net option costs.

When the strike prices within a spread position are the same, no margin is required.

Investors must decide for themselves how much margin risk they can comfortably tolerate. Many seasoned investors/traders actively compare their margin risk directly against the potential rewards contained within the trade. Others simply consider margin as one of the ordinary risks of trading. Generally, we have found that the amount of margin an individual can tolerate is directly related to the degree of confidence he has in the underlying stock of the option spread, as well as the limit of his available funds. We recommend that you develop your own tolerance, but once that level is established, stay firmly within the guidelines you have set for yourself. Personally, I wouldn't enter into an investment with a risk of losing $1,000.00, when the potential gains from that investment was only $100.00. However, if the potential gain was $500.00, and after considering other factors, I would more likely find the risk tolerable. Of course, peripheral factors should also be considered. Whatever you decide, manage your margin risk just as vigorously as any other risk in trading options. Risk and reward… You want those twins to work in your favor, so set your goals and stick to them.

The higher the risk, the more potential for greater rewards.

Consequently, we have divided our primary strategies into three overlapping categories determined by the volatility of the underlying stock:

- **Volatile**
- **Moderate**
- **Generally Static**

In the first example in the next chapter, the ABCD underlying stock is considered *Moderate*; meaning that while the stock's movement isn't radical, it is susceptible to occasional spikes in price. Stocks within the *Volatile* category can move as much as 10 to 30 points, or more, in a single day. Trading in this category is considered prudent for professional, day-traders only. The *Generally Static* category is reserved for underlying stocks which have a slow, predictable movement in share prices, or have no movement at all. This category is recommended for beginners and novice traders.

When our underlying stock picks make rapid and radical price swings, we rarely have the opportunity to allow our short options to expire. Instead, we buy back our short options before expiration, nailing down sure profits, then immediately sell the next month's option in order to continue our upward ride. Consider a six-stage rocket being launched into orbit. When the momentum of one stage has been exhausted, we jump to the next stage. As each used section is being jettisoned, getting rid of dead weigh, we are propelled steadily toward our goal. The *Moderate* category contains some elements of the other two categories. These stocks can have some price spikes, both up and down, while also being defined s somewhat slow and steady. Our last category of *Generally Static* stocks perhaps moves 2 to 4 points per month, if that. They can also have no movement at all. You can generally determine which category an option's underlying stock falls into by how often you are able to allow your short options to expire safely, vs. having to buy them back before expiration. Short options containing *Generally Static* stocks can almost always be allowed to expire at expiration, while options containing *Volatile* stocks will almost always need to be repurchased prior to expiration. Stocks falling into the *Generally Static* category would appeal to those who cannot spend a lot of time and effort monitoring the progress of their options on a daily basis. This category is defined by the slow rising, upward accumulation of profits, in strong hands.

Slow and steady profit gains enjoyed by those investors who are willing allow their options to expire each month, requiring little effort on their part.

Chapter 20: Option Profitability Trade Log

As with any growing and changing investment, <u>accurate bookkeeping is essential</u>. At any moment, your option positions should be readily available, and in a form that is easily understood. We highly recommend using the format of *Microsoft Office Excel* spreadsheet (or comparable software) as shown on our website: **www.800option.com**. <u>**Note: see our 2007 Track Record**</u>. For our purposes here, we recommend the following spreadsheet paradigm as a guideline for opening and closing all option trades. Feel free to make changes and additions to fit your needs and style.

<u>Data should be entered under the column headings listed below:</u>

- **Trade Date** – The date you make the trade.

- **# of Cont**. – the number of option contracts being bought or sold.

- **Stock** – The stock symbol for the underlying stock.

- **Call or Put** – The symbol of your choice can be entered into the Call or Put columns, indicating that particular type of option has been bought or sold. We prefer to use a checkmark, an X, or an asterisk (*).

- **Expire Month** is the 3rd Saturday of the month in which that particular option expires. At present there is no trading of options on Saturdays. Therefore, all expiring option trades for that month must be completed prior to close-of-market on the previous Friday.

- **Strike price** – In the event of exercise, the strike price is the price at which that option will be redeemed.

- **Cost purchase** – The price you paid to purchase an option, expressed in fractional or decimal form, i.e., 2 ¼, or 2.25. Use whichever form you prefer. The 2nd column under the same heading contains the total Cost of Purchase, <u>including commission</u>, expressed in dollar form.

- **Proceeds of sale** – The premium you received for selling an option, expressed in fractional or decimal form, i.e., 3 ¾, or 3.75. The 2nd column under the same heading contains the total Proceeds of the Sale, <u>excluding commission</u>, expressed in dollar form.

- **Profit and Loss** – Your gross profits, or losses, respectively. (<u>includes commissions</u>.)

- **Margin** – The amount of margin required to be set aside, by your brokerage, to cover associated risk, as determined by the strike price gap within the spread.

Each row of the Profitability Trade Log contains spaces for data entry pertaining to one complete turnaround of buying and selling the same option. <u>When first opening a new position by *buying* an option, entries should be placed as in the below, first row example.</u> We have chosen the arbitrary amount of $40.00 as trading fees for each transaction example.

Buy ABCD Nov 65 Puts.

This is the opening leg of the option. The closing leg will likely be completed by *selling* the same option sometime in November, and nearer to its expiration date. Entries into the remaining, empty boxes on the same row will be made at that time. In the next row example, the opening sale of the ABCD June 68 ½ Put option is depicted. The entries will not be completed until that option is eventually closed, either by repurchasing the same option before expiration, allowing it to expire on the 3rd Saturday in June, or it is exercised by the option owner.

On June 6th the ABCD stock price was $69.00. Our advisory service advised that ABCD stock would likely increase in value within the foreseeable future. Therefore, their recommendation was to first, purchase a long-term Put. Then, sell successive, monthly short-term Puts on the same stock. We followed their advice, and

Bought 5 contracts of ABCD November 65 Puts for 6.

$6.00 x 500 shares = $3,000.00 + $40.00 commission = $3,040.00.

Using these November, long-term Puts as a hedge, we then sell monthly, short-term Puts on the same stock.

Sold 5 contracts ABCD June 68 ½ Puts for a premium of 1.

$1.00 x 500 shares = $500.00 - $40.00 trading fee = $460.00 net premium received.

$3,040.00, cost of long option purchase - $460.00, premium received for short option sale = $2580.00 initial net spread debit. (See log entry below.)

YOUR OPTION PROFITABILITY TRADE LOG

Trade Date	# of Cont	Stock	Calls	Puts	Expire Month	Strike Price	Cost Purchase		Proceeds Of Sale		Margin	Profit	Loss
6/6/	5	ABCD		X	Nov	65	6	$3040.00					
6/6/	5	ABCD		X	June	68 1/2			1	$460.00	3 ½ $1750		

Because the strike price of the short option is greater than that of the long option, there is an inherent, un-hedged risk of 3 ½ points, or $3.50 per share x 500 shares = $1750.00. That risk is reflected within our margin account, and funds will be set aside t cover it. See Margin above.

The ABCD stock performed as expected. The stock price rose to $72.00 per share, and remained above the short option strike price. The option was not exercised, but expired, allowing us to capture the entire $460.00 premium as profit. However, in contrast to the $3,040.00 we paid for the opposing, long-term, Nov 65 Puts, this is a small profit indeed. Read on! It gets better.

After the ABCD June 68 ½ Put option expired, our long ABCD Nov 65 Put option remains in place, acting as a hedge against any other short-term ABCD Put options we wish to sell. Let's now complete our log entries. By allowing the ABCD June 68 ½ Puts to expire, the position was effectively closed, creating a profit of $460.00 and canceling our margin requirement. The act of expiration is considered a separate trade by our broker, and costs us an additional brokerage fee. That $40.00 trade fee is subtracted from our profit.

YOUR OPTION PROFITABILITY TRADE LOG

Trade Date	# of Cont	Stock	Calls	Puts	Expire Month	Strike Price	Cost	Purchase	Proceeds	Of Sale	Margin	Profit	Loss
6/6/	5	ABCD		X	Nov	65	6	$3040					
6/6/ 6/20/	5	ABCD		X	June	68 ½		Expired	1	$460		$420	

Note: Margin requirement is no longer necessary after expiration of the option, and is removed.

ABCD stock price is now $72.00 per share. Our next step is to immediately

Sell 5 contracts ABCD July 70 Puts for 3 ¼.

$3.25 x 500 shares = $1625.00 premium received - $40.00 commission = $1585.00. Since we purposely chose an ABCD Put option with a strike price of $70.00, we now have a 5-point margin requirement. In order to eliminate any margin requirement, we could have sold the July 65 Puts, instead of the July 70's, but they were only selling for 1, or $1.00. We felt the July 70 Puts were a better value. (See log entry.)

YOUR OPTION PROFITABILITY TRADE LOG

Trade Date	# of Cont	Stock	Calls	Puts	Expire Month	Strike Price	Cost Purchase		Proceeds Of Sale		Margin	Profit	Loss
6/6/	5	ABCD		X	Nov	65	6	$3040					
6/6/ 6/20/	5	ABCD		X	June	68 ½		Expired	1	$ 460		$420	
6/20/	5	ABCD		X	July	70			3 1/4	$1585	5 $2500		

Note: Margin requirement for the July 70 Puts is 5, or 5 X 500 shares = $2,500.00.
One week before July expiration, the ABCD stock price fell to $69.00, one

point below the strike-price of our short option. That price-drop rendered our option **ITM**, and has a greater chance of being exercised. However, since the purchaser of the option paid a premium to buy it, the ABCD stock would likely have to fall a point or two further before he could make even a modest profit by exercising the option. We also keep in mind that on expiration day many option brokerages automatically exercise **ITM** options, even if they are only **ITM** by a fraction of a point.

We decide to manage our risk once again by buying back the July 70 puts. This action nails-down considerable profits for us, while eliminating the risk of exercise.

Buy-back 5 contracts ABCD July 70 puts for 1 1/8.

1.125 X 500 = $562.50 + $40.00 trade fee = $602.50. Simultaneously, we

Sell 5 contracts ABCD August 70 puts for 3.

3 X 500 = $1500.00 - $40.00 trade fee = 1,460.00

Note: The ABCD stock price is $69.00, making the August 70 put option one point **ITM**. Normally, we would only sell options that are **OTM** to further hedge our risk against exercise. In this instance, our own research strongly indicates the ABCD stock price drop to $69.00 was only a temporary fall, and should soon rebound strongly. Therefore, we are satisfied the trade is safe. (See chart below.)

YOUR OPTION PROFITABILITY TRADE LOG

Trade Date	# of Cont	Stock	Calls	Puts	Expire Month	Strike Price	Cost	Purchase	Proceeds Of Sale		Margin	Profit	Loss
6/6/	5	ABCD		X	Nov	65	6	$3040					
6/6/ 6/20/	5	ABCD		X	June	68 ½		Expired	1	$ 460		$420	
6/20/ 07/15	5	ABCD		X	July	70	1 1/8	$602.50	3 1/4	$1585		$982.50	
07/15	5	ABCD		X	Aug	70			3	$1460	5	$2500	

By August expiration day, the ABCD stock price had risen to $81.00 per share. Our ABCD August 70 Put option expired.

YOUR OPTION PROFITABILITY TRADE LOG

Trade Date	# of Cont	Stock	Calls	Puts	Expire Month	Strike Price	Cost Purchase		Proceeds Of Sale		Margin	Profit	Loss
6/6/	5	ABCD		X	Nov	65	6	$3040					
6/6/ 6/20/	5	ABCD		X	June	68 1/2		Expired	1	$ 460		$420	
6/20/ 7/15/	5	ABCD		X	July	70	1 1/8	$602.50	3 1/4	$1585		$982.50	
7/15/ 8/21/	5	ABCD		X	Aug	70		Expired	3	$1460		$1420	

Note: Margin requirement has been released on the Aug 70 put option.

Intermediate Summary

Our initial, long option purchase cost was $3040.00. Our profits earned from selling short-term Puts, to date, is $420.00 + $982.50 + $1,420.00 = $2,822.50.

$3,040.00 debit - $2,822.50 = $217.50 net debit, so far.

Now, we have another risk management decision to make. The ABCD stock price is $81.00 per share. If we sell an ABCD September 80 Put, our margin requirement will jump to 15 points.

15 X 500 shares = $7,500.00. We might not have that much money to devote to margin requirements, or we simply do not want to take the risk of the stock price suddenly plummeting below $65.00 per share, and the option being exercised.

Our alternative:

Purchase 5 contracts ABCD February 80 Puts for 5.

5 X 500 = $2,500.00 + $40.00 trade fee = $2,540.00. We simultaneously,

Sell 5 contracts ABCD Sept 80 Puts for 3.

3 X 500 = $1,500.00 - $40.00 trade fee = $1,460.00 net premium received.

With the purchase of the long February 80 puts, we are beginning a new series of Put spreads. At this point, our profit has been minimal, but we are further reducing our debit, as well as our risk, with every trade we make. With the long February 80 Put option purchased, several factors have turned in our favor:

Although our profit to this point has been small, we do enjoy one.

We still own the original, long Dec 65 Put option, and it is completely paid for. We could sell it, but would get a very small price. It would be more valuable to us as a hedge against a catastrophic drop in the ABCD stock price. Also, In using our newly purchased Feb 80 Puts as a hedge, we have reduced, to zero, our margin requirement against the Sept 80 Puts we sold, along with our risk, while freeing up more funds for trades.

In addition, we have extended our hedge insurance from November, through February. (See chart for update.)

YOUR OPTION PROFITABILITY TRADE LOG

Trade Date	# of Cont	Stock	Calls	Puts	Expire Month	Strike Price	Cost Purchase		Proceeds Of Sale		Margin	Profit	Loss
6/6/	5	ABCD		X	Nov	65	6	$3040					
6/6/ 6/20/	5	ABCD		X	June	68 1/2		Expired	1	$ 460		$420	
6/20/ 7/15/	5	ABCD		X	July	70	1 1/8	$602.50	3 1/4	$1585		$982.50	
7/15/ 8/21/	5	ABCD		X	Aug	70		Expired	3	$1460		$1420	
8/21/	5	ABCD		X	Feb	80	5	$2540 new long					
8/21/	5	ABCD		X	Sept	80			3	$1460	0		

Note: The strike price of the September 80 short option is the same as the February 80 long option. Therefore, there is no margin requirement.

In September, the ABCD stock price was $82.00, allowing the September option to expire.

YOUR OPTION PROFITABILITY TRADE LOG

Trade Date	# of Cont	Stock	Calls	Puts	Expire Month	Strike Price	Cost Purchase		Proceeds Of Sale		Margin	Profit	Loss
6/6/	5	ABCD		X	Nov	65	6	$3040					
6/6/ 6/20/	5	ABCD		X	June	68 ½		Expired	1	$ 460		$420	
6/20/	5	ABCD		X	July	70	1 1/8	$602.50	3 1/4	$1585		$982.50	
7/15/ 8/21/	5	ABCD		X	Aug	70		Expired	3	$1460		$1420	
8/21/	5	ABCD		X	Feb	80	5	$2540 new long					
8/21/ 9/19/	5	ABCD		X	Sept	80		Expired	3	$1460	0	$1420	

We sold 5 contracts ABCD Oct 80 Puts for 2 ¾.

YOUR OPTION PROFITABILITY TRADE LOG

Trade Date	# of Cont	Stock	Calls	Puts	Expire Month	Strike Price	Cost	Purchase	Proceeds	Of Sale	Margin	Profit	Loss
6/6/	5	ABCD		X	Nov	65	6	$3040					
6/6/ 6/20/	5	ABCD		X	June	68 1/2		Expired	1	$ 460		$420	
6/20/ 7/15/	5	ABCD		X	July	70	1 1/8	$602.50	3 1/4	$1585		$982.50	
7/15/ 8/21/	5	ABCD		X	Aug	70		Expired	3	$1460		$1420	
8/21/	5	ABCD		X	Feb	80	5	$2540 new long					
8/21/ 9/19/	5	ABCD		X	Sept	80		Expired	3	$1460		$1420	
9/19/	5	ABCD		X	Oct	80			2 3/4	$1335	0		

October expiration: The ABCD stock was $85.00 per share. Our October short option expired.

We sold 5 contracts ABCD Nov 80 Puts for 2 5/8.

YOUR OPTION PROFITABILITY TRADE LOG

Trade Date	# of Cont	Stock	Calls	Puts	Expire Month	Strike Price	Cost Purchase		Proceeds Of Sale		Margin	Profit	Loss
6/6/	5	ABCD		X	Nov	65	6	$3040					
6/6/ 6/20/	5	ABCD		X	June	68 1/2	Expired		1	$ 460		$420	
6/20/ 7/15/	5	ABCD		X	July	70	1 1/8	$602.50	3 1/4	$1585		$982.50	
7/15/ 8/21/	5	ABCD		X	Aug	70	Expired		3	$1460		$1420	
8/21/	5	ABCD		X	Feb	80	5	$2540 new long					
8/21/ 9/19/	5	ABCD		X	Sept	80	Expired		3	$1460		$1420	
9/19/ 10/17/	5	ABCD		X	Oct	80	Expired		2 3/4	$1335		$1335	
10/17/	5	ABCD		X	Nov	80			2 5/8	$1272.50	0		

November expiration date: ABCD stock price $87.00. Our November short option expired.

We Sold 5 contracts ABCD Dec 85 Puts for 3 ½.

YOUR OPTION PROFITABILITY TRADE LOG

Trade Date	# of Cont	Stock	Calls	Puts	Expire Month	Strike Price	Cost	Purchase	Proceeds	Of Sale	Margin	Profit	Loss
6/6/	5	ABCD		X	Nov	65	6	$3040					
6/6/ 6/20/	5	ABCD		X	June	68 1/2	Expired		1	$ 460		$420	
6/20/ 7/15/	5	ABCD		X	July	70	1 1/8	$602.50	3 1/4	$1585		$982.50	
7/15/ 8/21/	5	ABCD		X	Aug	70	Expired		3	$1460		$1420	
8/21/	5	ABCD		X	Feb	80	5	$2540					
8/21/ 9/19/	5	ABCD		X	Sept	80	Expired		3	$1460		$1420	
9/19/ 10/17/	5	ABCD		X	Oct	80	Expired		2 3/4	$1335		$1295	
10/17/ 11/18/	5	ABCD		X	Nov	80	Expired		2 5/8	$1272.50		$1232.50	
11/18/	5	ABCD		X	Dec	85			3 ½	$1710	5		

Note: The premium we could get for the Dec 80 options was only 1 ½. Instead, we decided to increase our strike price spread, and sell the December 85 Put option for 3 ½. We now have a 5-point margin requirement.

A week before December expiration we decide to visit our sister in the wilds of the Colorado Mountains for Christmas. No phone, no computer. Before making the trip, we want to vacate our December, short option position. We buy-back the ABCD Dec 85 Put options for 1 point to close the position.

1 X 500 = $500.00 + $40.00 trade fee = $540.00. (Note entry below.)

A significant change has occurred in the ABCD stock price, which is now $86.50.

Also, our original, long Dec 65 option expired. We Sell the ABCD Jan 85 Puts for 3.

YOUR OPTION PROFITABILITY TRADE LOG

Trade Date	# of Cont	Stock	Calls	Puts	Expire Month	Strike Price	Cost Purchase		Proceeds Of Sale		Margin	Profit	Loss
6/6/	5	ABCD		X	Nov	65	6	$3040		Expired			$3080
6/6/ 6/20/	5	ABCD		X	June	68 ½		Expired	1	$ 460			$420	
6/20/ 7/15/	5	ABCD		X	July	70	1 1/8	$602.50	3 ¼	$1585			$982.50	
7/15/ 8/21/	5	ABCD	.	X	Aug	70		Expired	3	$1460			$1420	
8/21/	5	ABCD		X	Feb	80	5	$2540						
8/21/ 9/19/	5	ABCD		X	Sept	80		Expired	3	$1460			$1420	
9/19/ 10/17/	5	ABCD		X	Oct	80		Expired	2 3/4	$1335			$1295	
10/17/ 11/18/	5	ABCD		X	Nov	80		Expired	2 5/8	$1272.50			$1232.50	
11/18/ 12/16	5	ABCD		X	Dec	85	1	$540.	3 ½	$1710			$1170	
12/16/	5	ABCD		X	Jan	85			3	$1460		5		

The January option expires. We now have one more month to go before, our long, February 80 hedge-option expires. We sell 5 contracts ABCD Feb 85 Puts for 2 5/8.

YOUR OPTION PROFITABILITY TRADE LOG

Trade Date	# of Cont	Stock	Calls	Puts	Expire Month	Strike Price	Cost Purchase		Proceeds Of Sale		Margin	Profit	Loss
6/6/	5	ABCD		X	Nov	65	6	$3040		Expired			$3080
6/6/ 6/20/	5	ABCD		X	June	68 ½		Expired	1	$ 460			$420	
6/20/ 7/15/	5	ABCD		X	July	70	1 1/8	$602.50	3 ¼	$1585			$982.50	
7/15/ 8/21/	5	ABCD		X	Aug	70		Expired	3	$1460			$1420	
8/21/	5	ABCD		X	Feb	80	5	$2540.00						
8/21/ 9/19/	5	ABCD		X	Sept	80		Expired	3	$1460			$14.20	
9/19/ 10/17/	5	ABCD		X	Oct	80		Expired	2 ¾	$1335			$1295	
10/17/ 11/18/	5	ABCD		X	Nov	80		Expired	2 5/8	$1272.50			$1232.50	
11/18/	5	ABCD		X	Dec	85	1	$540.00	3 ½	$1710			$1170	
12/16/	5	ABCD		X	Jan	85		Expired	3 ¼	$1585			$1545	
1/20/	5	ABCD		X	Feb	85			2 3/8	$1147.50	5			

February 10: A market correction was in full force. The ABCD stock price fell to $81.00 per share and our Feb 85 option was exercised. We were assigned 500 shares of ABCD stock, and were required to pay $85.00 per share. We did not want to own the stock; therefore, we immediately re-sold it for the market price of $81.00 per share, $1.00 per share above our hedge-option strike-price.

Assignment: 500 shares ABCD stock at $85.00 per share. 500 X $85.00 = $42,500.00.

We immediately re-sold the 500 shares ABCD stock for $81.00 per share. 500 X $81.00 = $40,500.00. $42,500.00 - $40,500.00 = $2,000.00 loss due to the assignment. $2,000.00 + $40.00 assignment trade fee = $2,040.00. From the $2,040.00 loss of this assignment, we subtract the premium received from the original sale of the Feb 85 Put option: $2,040.00 -

$1,147.50 = $892.50, which represents our net loss on the Feb 85 Put option complete turnaround.

YOUR OPTION PROFITABILITY TRADE LOG

Trade Date	# of Cont	Stock	Calls	Puts	Expire Month	Strike Price	Cost Purchase		Proceeds Of Sale		Margin	Profit	Loss
6/6/	5	ABCD		X	Nov	65	6	$3040		Expired			$3080
6/6/ 6/20/	5	ABCD		X	June	68 ½		Expired	1	$ 460		$420	
6/20/ 7/15/	5	ABCD		X	July	70	1 1/8	$602.50	3 ¼	$1585		$982.50	
7/15/ 8/21/	5	ABCD		X	Aug	70		Expired	3	$1460		$1420	
8/21/	5	ABCD		X	Feb	80	5	$2540.00					
8/21/ 9/19/	5	ABCD		X	Sept	80		Expired	3	$1460		$14.20	
9/19/ 10/17/	5	ABCD		X	Oct	80		Expired	2 ¾	$1335		$1295	
10/17/ 11/18/	5	ABCD		X	Nov	80		Expired	2 5/8	$1272.50		$1232.50	
11/18/ 12/16/	5	ABCD		X	Dec	85	1	$540.00	3 ½	$1710		$1170	
12/16/ 01/20/	5	ABCD		X	Jan	85		Expired	3 ¼	$1585		$1545	
1/20/	5	ABCD		X	Feb	85		Exercise $2040.00	2 3/8	$1147.50	5		$892.50

Since we did not exercise our long, February 80 put options, we were able to sell them prior to expiration for 1/8, or $62.50 - $40.00 trade fee = $22.50.

YOUR OPTION PROFITABILITY TRADE LOG

Trade Date	# of Cont	Stock	Calls	Puts	Expire Month	Strike Price	Cost Purchase		Proceeds Of Sale		Margin	Profit	Loss
6/6/	5	ABCD		X	Nov	65	6	$3040		Expired			$3080
6/6/ 6/20/	5	ABCD		X	June	68 ½		Expired	1	$ 460		$420	
6/20/ 7/15/	5	ABCD		X	July	70	1 1/8	$602.50	3 ¼	$1585		$982.50	
7/15/ 8/21/	5	ABCD		X	Aug	70		Expired	3	$1460		$1420	
8/21/	5	ABCD		X	Feb	80	5	$2540.00					
8/21/ 9/19/	5	ABCD		X	Sept	80		Expired	3	$1460		$14.20	
9/19/ 10/17/	5	ABCD		X	Oct	80		Expired	2 ¾	$1335		$1295	
10/17/ 11/18/	5	ABCD		X	Nov	80		Expired	2 5/8	$1272.50		$1232.50	
11/18/ 12/16/	5	ABCD		X	Dec	85	1	$540.00	3 ½	$1710		$1170	
12/16/ 01/20/	5	ABCD		X	Jan	85		Expired	3 ¼	$1585		$1545	
1/20/	5	ABCD		X	Feb	85		Exercise $2040.00	2 3/8	$1147.50	5		$892.50
Total												$9525	$6490

Our ABCD option position is closed. Now, let's finish our calculations to determine our overall profit/loss. To do this, we simply add all entries in both the profit, as well as the loss columns, and subtract the lesser number from the greater number.

Profit column: $9,525.00

Debits: $6,490.00

Net Profit: $3,035.00

The entire sum of our own money used was in purchasing the original December 65 option for $3040 - $460 (The amount we received from simultaneously selling the June 68 1/2 option) = $2,580.00. The rest of the money we used was essentially **OPM (Other-People's-Money)**.

Our initial investment: $2,580.00

Our net profit from all of the spread positions we held: $3,035.00

Percentage of profit from our investment: 117.6%, over a nine month period.

Admittedly, every option spread-position will not capture such lofty percentage gains. Most option traders have experienced even better gains than the ones shown here, and have also experienced occasional losses of the same magnitude. If you are going to trade option contracts, you must set your mind to the fact that you will profit on some, and lose on others… it is inevitable. However, if you staunchly practice sound risk management, such as shown in these pages, your chances of experiencing greater profits, as well as smaller and fewer losses, is virtually a given. The entire process is considerably repetitive. The more you practice trading, the more proficient you will become. Soon, you will discover opportunities to better almost every trade by using time and opportunity as your risk management tools.

Due to market fluctuations, the number of actual option expirations will be fewer than shown in the examples and the number of buy-backs will normally be more. We used the above examples to highlight as many different scenarios as possible. The dynamics of your portfolio may be different.

Chapter 21: Maximizing Profit on Each Trade

When directing your broker to make an options trade "**At the market**," <u>the trade would be executed at the current market price, and at the earliest moment the trade could be executed on the floor of the exchange</u>. If time is an important factor, and you need to make the trade as soon as possible, then "**At the market**" is certainly the order you would want to place. However, in making an "**At the market**" trade, **you must be aware that the execution of your order will be made at the worst possible price for you**. If your time situation is not critical, then you can easily receive or pay a more favorable price for your trade. The prices of options, as well as stocks, fluctuate throughout the trading day, so by preparing your calculations in advance, you can save yourself hundreds of dollars within the extremes of the "**Bid**" and "**Ask**" prices listed.

<u>Buying</u>

The idea is simply a bartering technique: A seller wants to sell you an item for $1.00, and you don't want to pay but fifty cents. Somewhere in between the two values lies an equitable trade. From the **CBOE** option price-chart, determine the "*Ask*" price of an option you want to purchase, say it is 3 ½, then look for the "*Bid*" price for the same option... perhaps it is 3. You could go ahead and buy the option at the ask price of 3 ½, but you could also likely buy the option for some figure between the 3 ½ ask price, and the 3 bid price, saving you money. The ***middle ground*** is a figure the seller is willing to take for the option, and you, as a buyer, are willing to pay for it. If the underlying stock price of an option has been falling, rendering the value of that particular option worth less than if it were increasing in value, the floor trader might be willing to grab your price before the stock sinks any further. The listed option price ranges are: Ask 3 ½, and bid 3. The exact value between the two, the middle ground, is 3 ¼. In reality, you could enter an order with your broker to buy the option at 3 ¼, **GTC** (the order would continue in force until you cancelled it), "**Good 'Til Cancelled (GTC)**." Or you could make the order good for that trading day only (**A Day Order**). Then, as the price of the option fluctuates, and time erodes some of its value, it is possible your order would eventually be executed at your price. However, if the underlying stock price moves in the other direction, or your offered price simply has not been accepted, then you'll need to adjust your offer. Move your 3-¼ bid just slightly toward the seller's advantage, to 3 5/16, or even 3 3/8. In using this strategy, you determine the center between the bid and ask prices, then tilt that figure toward the opposing side's favor, ending with a very executable and attractive order position. When you become the *seller,* simply reverse the process.

Selling

Bid 3, ask 3 ½; the middle ground is 3 ¼. Since I am now *selling* the option, I want to sell it at the best possible price in my favor. I can hold to the *ask* price of 3 ½, offer the option at the middle ground of 3 ¼, or tilt the price even more in the *buyer's* favor, 3 3/16, or even 3 1/8. It is possible to execute the trade at any of the above values. However, the probability of execution increases, as the price becomes more attractive to the buyer. Remember, the floor trader is maneuvering in a similar manner, and will also attempt to capture the best possible price for himself.

Chapter 22: Spread Option Trades

Access the **Options Price Chart** located at the **CBOE** website, or any financial site containing option listings. <u>The chart will contain two distinct columns of figures, one for **Calls**, on the left, and the other for **Puts**, on the right side of the page.</u> Scan the figures listed, as well as what those figures represent: **Last Sale, Net, Bid, Ask, Volume (Vol.), Open Interest.** Note: Volume represents the number of contracts traded that particular session. Open Interest represents the number of contracts trades since inception. Continuing: Your intentions are to complete the following option spread:

Buy 10 contracts ABC November 35 Puts for... Simultaneously, you want to

Sell 10 contracts ABC July 37 ½ Puts for...

Find the ***middle ground*** between the bid and ask prices of the option you want to SELL.

ABC July 40 Put Bid 1.....Ask 1 ½. ***Sell side***, middle ground = 1 ¼.

Find the middle ground between the bid and ask prices of the option you want to BUY.

ABC Nov 35 Put Bid 2.... Ask 2 ½. ***Buy side***, middle ground = 2 ¼.

Subtract the smaller number from the larger number to get the final figure. **If the SELL figure is greater than the BUY figure, then the option can be traded for a <u>credit</u>. If the BUY figure is larger than the SELL figure, then the option must be traded at a <u>debit</u>.**

2¼ - 1 ¼ = 1 debit.

In this trade, the buy-side price was greater than the sell-side price; therefore, the trade must be made at a debit. **The figure or number "1" represents the net price difference between the asking price of the option you are selling, and the offering price of the option you want to buy**.

In the above example, the value of "1" also indicates that you want to simultaneously make **both** the **sale** of one option, and the **purchase** of another option, at a net debit of 1. The bid and ask prices for both options will constantly fluctuate in the market, but you don't really care. In placing your order to buy ABC November 35 Puts, and sell ABC July 40 Puts, together in a single transaction, you are telling the broker that you want to complete both transactions at a net debit of 1, regardless of the bid and ask prices at the time. This means you will make both trades for a maximum price-spread differential of 1. For fee purposes, you will be billed separately for both trades.

The above calculations should be used every time you make a trade, saving you hundreds, even thousands of dollars over time. However, if you need an immediate trade, then enter the spread transaction "**At the market**." In entering this order, you will buy the option at it's ask price, and sell the opposing option at its bid price at the time the order is executed. *(This can be an extremely expensive way to make trades.)* If you have more time to allow the fluctuations of the market to affect option prices, then use the calculation strategy above. A **word of caution** on the conservative side: **Do not allow yourself to get so caught up in bartering that you lose possible profit gains by trying to save 1/16 of a point on the trade**. If you believe the underlying stock of your option will move in an advantageous direction fairly soon, then capture that position as soon as possible. However, if the order can remain open for a few hours, or a few days, then add (or subtract) up to 1/8 of a point to, or from, the final figure. You will be surprised at how often your trade will be executed at your offered price.

If the final figure of "1" is a **debit**, then add 1/8 to it = 1 1/8, for a more attractive trade for the floor trader. The option spread should be entered as 1 1/8 debit. If the final figure of "1" is a **credit**, subtract 1/8 from it, 1 - 1/8 = 7/8. The option spread should be entered as 7/8 credit. In both cases, you are leaning your "Bid" price for the option in the floor trader's favor, while remaining under the actual bid, or ask, price.

There is one more system that could work in your favor, which involves less mathematical calculations. In using the above strategy to calculate a more realistic bid for an option, you should be aware of the movement of both the underlying stock value, as well as the option price value. Is the option value increasing, or decreasing? Perhaps you need your trade to be executed fairly soon, and place a marginally acceptable bid to buy an option whose price is increasing in value. As time passes, there would be less likelihood of your offer being accepted, due to the option's increasing value.

The gap between the real, rising value of the option, and your bid, would be continuously widening; therefore, your bid could possibly be a waste of time.

Within the "**Option Listings**" there is a column indicating the value of the *last sale* made of a particular option. As stated, it indicates the price at which the last trade involving that option was made. **In a sense, the "Last Trade" price is representative of the actual, true value of that option**. If you needed a fairly prompt trade, and wanted to ensure your price was at least close to the real market value of the option, then enter your bid at the *last sale* price. If you could devote more time, perhaps the rest of the day, to making the trade, then enter your bid on either side of the *last sale* price, slightly in your favor. This strategy should be used only when you are in a hurry, and cannot take the time to use recommended calculation techniques.

As you can readily see, there are many variables from which to choose. We all want the best possible prices for our trades; profit is the main reason we are here. **Through experience find the strategy and the value-range that works best for you, as well as for the broker who is actively taking your orders. Once you decide upon a strategy for making your trade calculations, keep a record of how much of a hedge you used, and how long it took for the trade to execute. Your own data will guide you in making necessary adjustments so you can become more effective in making trades. Test and sharpen your skills daily, if possible. The more you practice, the more proficient you will become. Of course, you want to execute the fastest possible trades, but also the most lucrative ones**.

Unfortunately, in some respects, you can make the best possible calculations for trading options, yet still not be able to execute your trades. The prices you enter could be fair, and even more than fair, and still you wait for the execution, which passes you by. We must trade using the availability of brokers and floor traders. At present, there just isn't a way around it, but as I write this, the system is changing. Very soon I expect to be able to make spread option trades using the Internet, and trading within an even more narrow range of ask and bid prices. Be aware that the actual person on the floor of the exchange, or sitting at his market-making computer, decides whether or not your trade is executed. He evaluates the bid and ask prices of every proposed option sale, or purchase. The money that person earns is directly related to the spreads between the bid and ask prices of the stocks, and options, he allows to be traded. If that spread is too narrow, or non-existent, then his commission is low. If he can hold off making a trade until that price-gap widens, then he makes more money. He wants you, the trader, to give up 1/16 or 1/8 of a point on your offer so he can profit more on your trade. This practice can be marginally unethical if taken beyond accepted parameters established by the exchanges, but it does occur. Of course floor traders should be allowed to profit on our trades… they work very hard at a highly stressful job. As with any position of power, however, abuse can sometimes occur.

I mention this to possibly curb future frustration when the trades you submit seem to be ignored. In some instances, trades submitted through one brokerage seem to be executed faster, and more often, than with other firms. Perhaps our calculations are slightly unreasonable. Maybe we submit an order just as the values on the option's board change. There can be any number of reasons a trade fails to execute. You should be aware of them all. When you submit a trade that doesn't execute, for any reason, you are at risk of the situation changing. A risk, not only from losing money on the proposed trade, but incurring possible further losses as the option you intended to purchase, increases in value while you are waiting for your trade to be executed; another form of risk management.

Below is a conversion table you will need to make your calculations, as well as entering data into the **Profitability Trade Log**.

Conversion table

1/16................... 0.0625

1/8.................... 0.125

3/16.................. 0.1875

¼...................... 0.25

5/16.................. 0.3125

3/8.................... 0.375

7/16.................. 0.4375

½...................... 0.50

9/16.................. 0.5625

5/8.................... 0.625

11/16................ 0.6875

¾..................... 0.75

13/16............... 0.8125

7/8.................. 0.875

15/16.............. 0.9375

Chapter 23: Making Live Trades

When making application to your selected brokerage firm, you will be asked for your trading history involving both stocks and options. Do not allow your lack of direct experience to deter you from completing the application. Requirements vary between brokerages. Some require prior experience in option trading, while others are satisfied that a professional advisor will monitor your trading. While these are legitimate concerns, there is a Catch 22 element at work. If you aren't allowed to trade options, then how do you acquire experience? Your broker wants your option trading experience to be positive and profitable for you, as well as for them. Because of the nature of option trading, if you were to get into trouble without the benefit of an outside advisor, the brokerage could be cast into the tenuous position of having to liquidate your existing positions, with no regard for the health of those assets. They will not offer, nor will they give, any trading advice. At least until you gain a modicum of experience, novice traders should consider acquiring the services of a professional advisor before risking cash in any option position.

While it is possible to trade options using the Internet, due to their inherent complexity, most spread-option orders must be placed over the telephone. I've experienced a time period as long as fifteen minutes for a broker to complete a single option spread order, while others have completed the same order in less than one minute. This time disparity seems mostly due to the experience level of the broker. Stock, options, and futures trading has become so widespread within the last few years that brokerages have had to recruit, train, and place their agents as quickly as possible. This leaves little time, or opportunity, for a thorough understanding involving all of the facets of complex trading. Those who develop a solid understanding of option trading are in very select company.

Having read this book, you already know more about options than most broker-agents you will encounter.

Let's go through the mechanics of a few typical trades with your broker. First, determine exactly what option position you want to open. After completing the necessary research, or upon consultation with your advisor, you decide you want to open a Put spread on ABCD stock. You want to purchase one contract of ABCD Puts, expiring six months in the future. Simultaneously, you want to sell one contract of ABCD Puts, expiring next month. In checking the **CBOE** web site, you determine that ABCD stock is selling for $20.00 per share. The date is January 25th, and the

June 20 Puts are selling for: Bid 3 ¾. Ask 4.

The February 20 Puts are selling for: Bid 1 ½. Ask 1 ¾.

You want to place the order as a spread position. (Ref. Chapter 9) Now it is time to do the math.

June 20 Puts: Bid 3 ¾ Ask 4.

You determine the middle ground between the two prices is 3 7/8.

The February 20 Puts are selling for: Bid 1 ½. Ask 1 ¾.

The middle ground here is 1 5/8.

By subtracting the smaller number from the larger number, you get 2 ¼. Since the purchase-price of 3 7/8 is greater than the selling price of 1 5/8, the price we might offer for the spread is a 2-¼ debit. (To ensure prompt execution, let's consider increasing our offer to 2 3/8 debit.)

Upon reaching your broker by phone, the conversation should go something like this: (**Note: Some brokerages state they are recording all transactions; others do not**.) The broker will ask you for your account number along with various, other information to verify your identity. You tell the broker that you want to open a "**Put spread option position**". He should tell you to go ahead.

"I want to buy one contract ABCD June 20 Puts (pause), and sell one contract ABCD February 20 Puts, to open, for a 2 3/8 debit. The order is "**Good Til Cancelled**." (**Note: Some brokerages won't accept GTC orders for spread positions; therefore, they will be placed as Day orders**.) At this point, the broker will likely ask you to wait for a moment while he writes the order by hand. He will also likely ask you to repeat parts of the order. There may be more pauses, then, when he is ready he will read the order back to you for your confirmation. After you confirm the order, he will ask if you have another trade. If not, your business is concluded.

Some brokerages will ask for your phone number and call you when the trade has been executed. Others will not; in which case you must call them. <u>Enter as much of the information as possible into the **Profitability Trade Log**</u>. Even though these two option orders were placed simultaneously, they are separate orders and must be logged as such. Enter the Buy order information for the June 20 Puts on one row, and the sell order for the February 20 Puts on the line directly below it. Do not enter "Purchase" or "Selling" prices at this time. As yet, you do not know those exact values.

Hopefully soon, your broker will call with a "Fill" notification. He should use language similar to the following: "You bought one contract ABCD June 20 Puts for 3 5/8, and sold one contract ABCD February 20 Puts for 1 1/4". That is a spread debit of 2 3/8. (Note that the sell price changed, but the overall spread debit remained the same as offered.) 3 5/8 – 1 ¼ = 2 3/8 debit.

Be certain to jot down the buy and sell values he gives you, then enter them into the **Profitability Trade Log** spreadsheet. **My strong suggestion is to make your entries using a #2 lead pencil** (if you are keeping a physical handwritten record instead of computer file spreadsheet; which can be printed). Multiply the purchase price decimal value of (3 5/8) 3.625 X 100 shares = $362.50. Then do the same with the selling price of (1 ¼) 1.25 X 100 shares = $125.00. This will complete the first half of the entries necessary for both trades.

Subsequent spread trades should be made in the same manner; always selling one option to open a new position, while buying another one back, to close the old position. The situation does sometimes occur when you would want to buy back your short position (or after the short position expires), leaving the long option in place. Later, you would sell another short option to once again complete the spread. This maneuver is called "**Legging in**." In placing a "**Leg-in**" order, you simply tell the broker what you want to do.

"I want to leg-in and complete an open spread position on ABCD June 20 Puts. I want to sell one contract ABCD March 20 Puts for 1 ½," (or whatever price you are offering).

Occasionally, you will be asked questions about your order that you might not understand. When that happens, simply ask the broker to explain further. As long as you understand the basic fundamentals contained in this book, you should be able to complete any trade. The more trades you make, the more proficient you will inevitably become. There is no substitute for experience. Do not allow the broker to fluster you. If he asks questions you do not understand, and he seems impatient, cancel the order pertaining to the question and consult your advisor. Then armed with more information, place the order again. Most brokers will help you as much as possible with trade-specifics, but cannot offer investment advice.

The strategies contained in this book, as well as timing and order placement, will all become routine after a few trades. Learn all you can about option trading from other perspectives. Ask questions of your advisor, as well as your broker. If our guidelines for placing orders seem awkward to your broker, ask him to spell out exactly how he wants the order placed. He will be happy to tell you. It is important for both you and your broker to be completely comfortable and concise in your dealings. I have dealt with no less than four different brokerage firms within the past year, searching for the perfect system. I've liked parts of each one tried, but the perfect system eludes me. Either the cost is too high, or I can't seem to get the trades I need, when I need them. Whatever the reason, I always tell the brokerage what I like and what I don't like about their service, or the system they are using. After all, how can they improve without feedback from their customers?

What determines the price of an option? Pure and simple, supply vs. demand; buyers vs. sellers. If there are all buyers, and few sellers, it is the responsibility of the floor market-makers (Knight, etc.) to make the market. These guys are no angels. They are not altruistic. They are out to profit from buyers who place market orders for their options. That is why the **Option Clearing Corporation** has established 3 competing market-makers on 3 exchanges. Hopefully, a good brokerage house will shop the market and get the best price for you. That is why we give you specific debits and credits for your spreads. That is also why you may not get some orders filled. Because the market-makers see you coming and move the market, that is, another reason why our Sharp TM 20 device will alert you during the day, so you can act on a timely basis.

Let's compare premiums on 2 stocks, CORL (20 3/8), and ROV (21 7/8).

A CORL Feb 20 **Call** can be presently bought for 3 3/8.

It is only 3/8 **In-The-Money (ITM)**. Therefore there exists 3 points of time premium for less than 1 month. If you bought the stock on margin, sold the

Call and the stock remained at 20 or rose, your investment would be $700 plus commissions per 100. Your return would be $ 337.50 less commissions a 48% profit in 1 month.

A ROV Feb 20 **Call** can be bought for 3 1/8 and is 1 7/8 **In-The-Money (ITM)**. The time premium is only 1 1/4. A better deal for the buyer, and a much less profitable deal for the seller.

I guess more investors think CORL will rise in 1 month, than ROV, or maybe the market-makers are exploiting the situation. Maybe CORL is more volatile than ROV?

I hope this comparison enhances your understanding of why you don't always receive executions on your limit orders. You must outsmart the market-makers, and not show your hand. Keep your aces in the hole when playing poker.

Note:

It merits mentioning that when dealing with any **In-The-Money (ITM) short Put <u>assignments</u>** you have 2 choices:

<u>Choice # 1</u>:

1. Keep the stock which you bought at a discount to the extent of the premium received when it was sold.

2. Sell a covered Call on the stock at a strike price just above the present price of the stock.

<u>Choice # 2</u>:

Sell the stock (day trade) and sell the next consecutive month Put at a strike price equal or above the strike price of the long Put owned.

Which method that you choose depends on the size of your portfolio and available capital funds.

Chapter 24: About Ascent Option Spreads

Regardless of the type of stock market in force at any given time, i.e., volatile, sluggish, bull, or bear, we make money in every possible trading climate. We advocate using **Put** and Call **calendar spreads** to protect existing portfolios against downside risk. We recommend selling hedged, short-term puts and calls, holding them until time causes the option to decay in value, then repurchase them at a greatly reduced price, or simply allow them to expire. Buy longer term, **Out-of-The-Money (OTM)** puts or calls (expiring 5 to 7 months in the future), and sell successive, short-term puts, or Calls, each month. The premiums received from selling short-term options reduce the cost of risk insurance (the long-term puts), which protect the portfolio from possible loss. The objective is to hold these positions until they reach the desired level, before selling, and not worry about a downside movement in the underlying stock, in the event of a market drop.

This strategy requires a minimum capital investment, while using **Other-People's-Money (OPM)** to compound profits, and further protect our portfolio. Time aggressively works against the *short-term option buyers*, as their options decay more in value with each passing day. In contrast, we hedge our short, sold-positions by purchasing long-term puts on the same underlying stock. The objective is to reduce the cost basis of our investment to zero, then, capture successive monthly premiums by selling more short-term puts each month. This strategy advocates buying the short-term puts back at a greatly reduced price, or allowing them to expire. Either way, profits can be substantial.

We are capitalizing on speculator's greed to increase wealth quickly. We recommend a more conservative, consistent rate of growth, with a high rate of return on investments. Visualize *buying* a whole chocolate pie for $5.00 (the long term puts), then *selling* each of the pie's 8 slices for $1.00 (the short term puts). $8.00 profit - $5.00 debit = $3.00 net profit, or 60%.

You can buy options at anytime, but they will all expire on the 3rd Saturday of the given month. You can,

Choose to buy options with expirations several months in the future.

- **Sell options at the same strike price for a shorter time interval**.
- **Replicate these sales until your original hedge-option expires**.
- **Trade options simultaneously via electronic trading, or with a broker**.

Consider your long-term Put, or Call, as a 6 to 8 months license to operate a casino. It allows you to capture short-term premiums; money that gamblers continuously give to you in attempting to beat the odds by speculating they will make profits on very risky bets. They feverishly feed the slot machines, ante up at poker, double-down on blackjack, or spin the roulette wheel. The odds are overwhelmingly against these short-term buyers. You, as the casino owner, continuously capture these short-term premiums, easily offsetting the expense of the license to operate the casino, then earning substantial, clear profits in the following months. They know the odds are with the casino owner, but they still take the enormous gamble on the slim chance they will hit a jackpot. The lottery works in the same manner.

On one side of the position, the transaction is definitely gambling, while on the other, the casino is simply engaging in business. Would you rather bet on the remote chance of a gambler's rare, limited success, or rake in the steady, routine premiums captured from operating a successful business? Yes, occasionally a gambler does beat the odds to enjoy a limited, windfall return on his bet. For the casino owner, that is simply part of the cost of doing business. But we all know where the true, long-term profits lie. 30%, 40%, 50% and more, are common, and in short periods of time. The odds are with the short-term option seller, not the buyer.

The trading strategies contained in this book have been used successfully by me (Don Shapray) for nearly 28 years. My option trading advice has literally helped clients make fortunes. I have been the CEO of my own option trading advisory service for at least the past 22 years, or longer. One of my websites, outlining available advisory plans, can easily be found on the Internet at **www.800option.com**. Information concerning "Case Studies," "Past Performance," as well as specific and overall strategies can also be accessed from the web site. If you would like to speak with me (Don), personally, **call 1-866-6-SPREAD (777323) during stock market hours. I would be more than happy to discuss my strategies, or the services my organization offers**.

Also, "I firmly believe that no one else has such a complete understanding of these strategies, or can better advise how to use them to make money. As in many instances, success depends not only on the strategies themselves, but on how, and when, to apply them. Personally, I put considerable trust in an advisor's own track record. **Ascent Option Spreads**' track record is available on their web site, and is open for all to inspect. Don is proud of it, and rightfully so. We strongly recommend that you keep track of your trading record, as well. Past performance is an excellent indicator of how you are doing... and how **Ascent Option Spreads** is doing." (Paul Ellsworth)

Chapter 25: Option Strategies

You will discover the great majority of occurrences, requiring action on your part, are repetitive, while some other potentially damaging events only surface occasionally. You must be aware, not only of these potential problems, but also of specific action to take to protect your investments. Of course your main objective is to profit from the situation. We thought it would be helpful to exemplify how we have handled some of these situations within our own portfolios. We believe strongly in preparation for an event which, left untended, could have a negative effect on any option portfolio. Once the situation is upon us, immediate action may be necessary to avoid negative consequences. Know what action to take *before* the event occurs. This is one of the chief reasons we advocate maintaining a close relationship with an options advisor. When in doubt… ask a professional.

Situation: What happens when a stock declines sharply in response to an overreaction to news that doesn't really affect its fundamentals? Consider the situation with VISX, a maker of optical laser surgical devices. The position for the initial spread was:

Bought June 75 Puts and

Sell Dec 80 Puts for a 6-¾ debit.

A court handed down an adverse decision pertaining to VISX laser surgical device patents, causing the stock to drop from 76 ¾ to 48 ¾. Depending upon your margin spread, this drop in stock price could have major consequences to your option position.

Strategy: At the height of its volatility, the VISX June 75 Puts could be sold for 30, or $3,000.00 per option contract, while simultaneously buying Jan 50 Puts as an interim, hedge-protection measure, in case VISX stock price were to fall further. When the stock rallies back up to its normal level, the position could be reversed, whereas the Jan 50 Puts could be sold, and the June 75 Puts repurchased for less money. In this situation, some would immediately try to protect their position by purchasing Calls, based on the stock's new, lower price, or even purchasing the stock outright. Perhaps, but our strategy offers more risk management, as purchasing the stock outright would be quite expensive, and we'd be gambling that the stock price would actually rise.

Purchasing a Call on VISX, as we have learned in previous chapters, has serious time limitations, plus the fact that Calls are normally more expensive than Puts, especially during a bull market.

(The above mentioned June 75 Puts, were actually advertised on the **CBOE** website for 30, or $3,000.00 per contract, during this VISX volatility period.) Most investors would view this period of VISX volatility as a highly negative occurrence, even scary, while we saw enormous opportunity for profit. The key is having a preconceived plan, while having the knowledge and understanding to implement it successfully.

Our strategy worked very well in the case of INTU when the chairman resigned, and the stock dropped 29 7/8 to 22. INTU was shortly thereafter selling for 57 ¼. The same scenario applies to VO (Seagrams), dropping to 36, then, bouncing back to 48 within a short time frame.

The following is a collective spreadsheet depicting the actual option history of INTU (Intuit) during a recent period. This underlying option stock is considered to be within the *Volatile* category. Please follow along with each transaction. Each new row on the log-chart is a separate entry. (Trading fees are not included within these calculations.) Note the use of "B" and "S" in the Put columns. Feel free to use these to indicate "Bought" and "Sold," or simply use an asterisk.

I opened my position by purchasing 5 contracts INTU Jan 28 5/8 Puts for 4 ¾, and selling 5 contracts INTU Nov 28 5/8 Puts for 2 7/8. No margin required.

YOUR OPTION PROFITABILITY TRADE LOG

Trade Date	# of Cont	Stock	Calls	Puts	Expire Month	Strike Price	Cost Purchase		Proceeds Of Sale		Margin	Profit	Loss
10/27/99	5	INTU		B	JAN	28 5/8	4 ¾	2375					
10/27/99	5	INTU		S	NOV	28 5/8			2 7/8	1437.50	0		

Below, I bought-back the INTU Nov 28 5/8 Puts for ½, and sold INTU Dec 35 Puts for 4 ¾. I now have a margin requirement of $3,187.50.

YOUR OPTION PROFITABILITY TRADE LOG

Trade Date	# of Cont	Stock	Calls	Puts	Expire Month	Strike Price	Cost Purchase		Proceeds Of Sale		Margin	Profit	Loss
10/27/99	5	INTU		B	JAN	28 5/8	4 ¾	2375					
10/27/99 11/07/99	5	INTU		S B	NOV	28 5/8	½	250	2 7/8	1437.50	0	1187.50	
11/07/99	5	INTU		S	DEC	35			4 ¾	2375	3187.50		

I bought-back the INTU Dec 35 Puts for 3 11/16, and sold the Jan 31 5/8 for 2 ¾. I now have a margin requirement of $1,500.00. (See chart below.)

YOUR OPTION PROFITABILITY TRADE LOG

Trade Date	# of Cont	Stock	Calls	Puts	Expire Month	Strike Price	Cost Purchase		Proceeds Of Sale		Margin	Profit	Loss
10/27/99	5	INTU		B	JAN	28 5/8	4 3/4	2375					
10/27/99 11/07/99	5	INTU		S B	NOV	28 5/8	½	250	2 7/8	1437.50		1187.50	
11/07/99 11/12/99	5	INTU		S B	DEC	35	3 11/16	1843.75	4 ¾	2375	0	531.25	
11/12/99	5	INTU		S	JAN	31 5/8			2 ¾	1375	1500		

At this point, the INTU stock price was rising very fast, soaring above the $38.00 mark. I saw an opportunity to buy back my Jan 31 5/8 Puts for 1 5/16, a significant profit. Then simultaneously sell a Jan 36 5/8 Put for 2 11/16, a nice premium… all within the same month. My margin requirement has grown to $4,000.00. (See chart below.)

YOUR OPTION PROFITABILITY TRADE LOG

Trade Date	# of Cont	Stock	Calls	Puts	Expire Month	Strike Price	Cost Purchase		Proceeds Of Sale		Margin	Profit	Loss
10/27/99	5	INTU		B	JAN	28 5/8	4 ¾	2375					
10/27/99 11/07/99	5	INTU		S B	NOV	28 5/8	1/2	250	2 7/8	1437.50		1187.50	
11/07/99 11/12/99	5	INTU		S B	DEC	35	3 11/16	1843.75	4 3/4	2375	0	531.25	
11/12/99 11/22/99	5	INTU		S B	JAN	31 5/8	1 5/16	656.25	2 3/4	1375	0	748.75	
11/22/99	5	INTU		S	JAN	36 5/8			2 11/16	1343.75	4000		

YOUR OPTION PROFITABILITY TRADE LOG

Trade Date	# of Cont	Stock	Calls	Puts	Expire Month	Strike Price	Cost Purchase		Proceeds Of Sale		Margin	Profit	Loss
10/27/99 11/22/99	5	INTU		*	JAN	28 5/8	4 ¾	2375					
10/27/99 11/07/99	5	INTU		*	NOV	28 5/8	½	250	2 7/8	1437.50		1187.50	
11/07/99 11/12/99	5	INTU		*	DEC	35	3 11/16	1843.75	4 3/4	2375	0	531.25	
11/12/99 11/22/99	5	INTU		*	JAN	31 5/8	1 5/16	656.25	2 3/4	1375	0	748.75	
11/22/99 11/22/99	5	INTU		*	JAN	36 5/8	¾	375	2 11/16	1343.75	0	968.75	

On November 22, 1999, the INTU stock was very volatile, causing me to radically change my positions. At the same time, I bought back my January 31 5/8 short Puts, closing that position. I also saw an excellent opportunity to sell my original, long January 28 5/8 Puts for a handsome profit. Since I then needed a long Put option as a hedge against my short positions, I purchased long April 31 5/8 Puts, while simultaneously selling the short January 36 5/8 Puts. With this transaction, I exercised two important strategies: First, I lessened my margin requirement from $4,000.00, to an adjusted $2,500.00. Secondly, I extended the limits of my spread option hedge protection from January to April, all while realizing considerable profits and reducing my exposure to risk. (See spreadsheet log below.) Note the full turnaround and closure of my original long January 28 5/8 position (First row.)

YOUR OPTION PROFITABILITY TRADE LOG

Trade Date	# of Cont	Stock	Calls	Puts	Expire Month	Strike Price	Cost Purchase		Proceeds Of Sale		Margin	Profit	Loss
10/27/99 11/22/99	5	INTU		* *	JAN	28 5/8	4 ¾	2375	1 1/8	560			1815
10/27/99 1/07/99	5	INTU		* *	NOV	28 5/8	½	250	2 7/8	1437.50	0	1187.50	
11/07/99 11/12/99	5	INTU		* *	DEC	35	3 11/16	1843.75	4 3/4	2375	0	531.25	
11/12/99 11/22/99	5	INTU		* *	JAN	31 5/8	1 5/16	656.25	2 3/4	1375	0	748.75	
11/22/99	5	INTU		B	April	31 5/8	4 ¼	2125.					
11/22/99	5	INTU		S	Jan	36 5/8			2 11/16	1343.75	2500.		

The INTU stock price was rising so rapidly, that just four days after selling the INTU Jan 36 5/8 Puts, I was able to buy them back at an excellent profit, while simultaneously selling April 50 Puts.

YOUR OPTION PROFITABILITY TRADE LOG

Trade Date	# of Cont	Stock	Calls	Puts	Expire Month	Strike Price	Cost Purchase		Proceeds Of Sale		Margin	Profit	Loss
10/27/99 11/22/99	5	INTU		*	JAN	28 5/8	4 ¾	2375	1 1/8	560			1815
10/27/99 11/07/99	5	INTU		*	NOV	28 5/8	1/2	250	2 7/8	1437.50	0	1187.50	
11/07/99 11/12/99	5	INTU		*	DEC	35	3 11/16	1843.75	4 3/4	2375	0	531.25	
11/12/99 11/22/99	5	INTU		*	JAN	31 5/8	1 5/16	656.25	2 3/4	1375	0	748.75	
11/22/99	5	INTU		B	April	31 5/8	4 ¼	2125.					
11/22/99 11/26/99	5	INTU		*	JAN	36 5/8	¾	375	2 11/16	1343.75	0	968.75	
11/26/99	5	INTU		S	April	50			6 1/8	3062.50	9187.50		

You well might ask why I sold April options on INTU, while still in November, skipping the months of December, January, February, and March. I did this for two reasons: First, the enormous premium I received for the April 50 Puts was better than what was quoted for the other three months combined. Secondly, Y2K loomed ominously over the market at that time, making any further growth in the INTU stock during the rest of 1999, and the first couple of months in 2000, questionable. I decided to manage my risks once again, and protect my profits. It so happened that on December 12, I was able to buy back the April 50 Puts and realize a substantial profit on the short-term position. I simultaneously sold an April 55 Put option, capturing even greater premium value. (See chart below.)

YOUR OPTION PROFITABILITY TRADE LOG

Trade Date	# of Cont	Stock	Calls	Puts	Expire Month	Strike Price	Cost Purchase		Proceeds Of Sale		Margin	Profit	Loss
10/27/99 1/22/99	5	INTU		*	JAN	28 5/8	4 ¾	2375	1 1/8	560			1815
10/27/99 11/07/99	5	INTU		*	NOV	28 5/8	½	250	2 7/8	1437.50	0	1187.50	
11/07/99 11/12/99	5	INTU		*	DEC	35	3 11/16	1843.75	4 3/4	2375	0	531.25	
11/12/99 11/22/99	5	INTU		*	JAN	31 5/8	1 5/16	656.25	2 3/4	1375	0	748.75	
11/22/99	5	INTU		B	April	31 5/8	4 ¼	2125.					
11/22/99 11/26/99	5	INTU		*	JAN	36 5/8	¾	375	2 11/16	1343.75	0	968.75	
11/26/99 12/07/99	5	INTU		S	APRIL	50	4 5/8	2312.50	6 1/8	3060	0	747.50	
12/07/99	5	INTU		S	April	55			7 5/16	3656.25	11687.50		

This option spread will not be closed until I buy back the April 55 Puts, or on April expiration day, whichever comes first. On 12/07/99, the INTU stock price was 62 ½. Do the math on this real- life spread and see for yourself the realized gains that are possible. Granted, these positions on Intuit stock are considered volatile, and the stock's movement bears that out, but it serves as a realistic example of what can be accomplished using superb stock picking, as well as good risk management strategies.

Appendix 1: Basics of Option Trading

Frequently Asked Questions (FAQ) -

Essential and little known facts:

- **WHAT IS AN OPTION?**

An Option is the right, but not the obligation, to purchase or sell a stock at a specified price, called a strike price, for a specific period of time until expiration date.

- **WHAT IS A CALL OPTION?**

A call option gives the holder the right to purchase a specified quantity of the underlying stock at a specified strike price by a specified expiration date.

- **WHAT IS A PUT OPTION?**

A put option gives the holder the right to sell a specified quantity of the underlying stock at a specified strike price by a specified expiration date.

- **HOW DOES AN OPTION TRADE WORK?**

Example: An issuer sells a call option, granting the holder the right to purchase 100 shares of a specific stock at $50 per share by a specified expiration date. At expiration date, if this stock is trading at $47.00, the holder would not exercise the option because there would it would not be prudent to pay $50 for a stock that is worth $47.

However, if at expiration date the stock price is $54.00, the call option holder could purchase 100 shares of the stock, now worth $5,400.00, for only $5,000.00.

- **WHAT IS THE PREMIUM RELATING TO AN OPTION?**

The premium is the price paid for the option. The premium is a factor of the intrinsic value of the option (the difference between the current price of the stock and the strike price) and the time value premium (the value that a speculator is willing to pay for the possible performance of the option until it expires). The time value premium lessens as time approaches expiration, to the point of zero on expiration date.

- **HOW IS MY INVESTMENT PROTECTED COMPARED TO HIGH RISK OPTION TRADES?**

The time value premium is a direct function of the volatility factor that we analyze with computer modeling of historical price performance, <u>THIS IS THE FUNDAMENTAL PREMISE OF OUR INVESTMENT STRATEGY</u>. By writing (or selling) call options with high volatility factors for short-term periods, our clients capture excess time value premiums which erode away from the buyer, and accrue to our clients as time approaches expiration date.

- **HOW DOES THE "YOUR OPTION STRATEGY" PROTECT AGAINST A PRICE RISE IN THE UNDERLYING STOCK?**

The client protects against a price rise by buying a long-term call option with a strike price above the current selling price of the underlying stock. Computer modeling will determine the theoretical value of said call option. We search for undervalued long term call options (9 or 10 month options) with sophisticated computer analysis.

- **WHY IS THIS STRATEGY PROFITABLE FOR OUR CLIENTS?**

This is profitable because buying short-term call options give speculators extreme percentage leverage on an upward price movement in the underlying stock. This is fine if you have a crystal ball to predict a short-term, upward price move. Nobody is that astute that they can make such a prediction with accuracy. We take the other side of the transaction by advocating you SELL (write) this short-term call option, instead. If the stock price rises, our client is perfectly hedged, and both parties profit. (Please refer to our CASE STUDIES for price charts.) If the stock price remains static, our clients profit by lowering their cost basis in the call option that they own. If their cost is lowered to zero, or produce a credit, by following this procedure for several periods, the profits can be substantial.

- **IF THIS STRATEGY IS SO PROFITABLE WHY DOESN'T EVERY INVESTOR USE IT?**

First:

Most investors are impatient for a greater and faster return on their investment, this being a 100+ percent return in less then one year. However, as stated previously on this site, "Banks and major corporate pension plans use conservative investments in options to balance their portfolios". This conservative investment is not a get-rich-quick plan or silver bullet. It produces a simple, steady return on your investment over time. We tell our clients: "Let the other guy gamble and take the risks, stay with the sure bet, and win."

Second:

Most investors don't have the tools or expertise to successfully use these sophisticated techniques. Our staff has over 30 years of experience in using these strategies. We've witnessed both bull and bear markets and can make worthwhile returns on investments, regardless of market performance.

- **"I have a portfolio of NASDAQ stocks that is down 57% from last year's high. I don't want to take such a huge loss by selling my stocks, but I'm not sure when, or if, they will recover to former levels."**

You are correct in your assessment. The best strategy is to dollar cost average by implementing an out of the money neutral put Calendar Spread. By that, I mean the following:

Buy a long-term, 4 or 5-month duration Put, and lower your cost basis by selling a short-term (1 month) Put at the same strike price, thereby recovering part of the cost of the long-term Put. If the stock price remains unchanged, drops to the strike price, or rises, you will pocket the full premium, and the process of selling consecutive 1 month Puts can be repeated until your long Put expires. This will lower the cost of the long-term put further, in many cases bringing it to zero, or producing a credit, in which case you enjoy a free ride for 2 or 3 months. Sell high and buy back at a lower price is just as profitable as buy low and sell high. It's the same thing.

- ## What happens if the stock price continues to fall?

The value of your long-term Put will continue to increase, and your short term Put will also increase, but not as much on an absolute numerical basis. (A smaller number such as 1 will represent a 100% increase to 2, whereas 4 must increase to 8 to represent a 100% increase). Of course, the options will both increase close to point-for-point as the stock price continues to fall below the strike price. Therein lies the limited risk of the trade. Limited to the original debit, less any time premium earned by the passage of time that has been captured by you as the spread seller (writer). However, the risk is much less than holding devalued stock.

- ## What happens if the put you sold is exercised? Do I have to put up the money to buy the stock?

No, as long as you sell the stock out the same day that the Put is exercised and sell the next consecutive month Put, it will not cost you any investment dollars. You will have made a profit, because you received a premium when you wrote the Put, which has lowered the cost of the stock Put to you.

> **Example:** **(Stock does not perform as expected.)** On Jan 10 ABC is selling for $30. You buy a put on ABC expiring on 3rd Friday of May at a strike price of $30 for $3.00. You simultaneously sell a put expiring on 3rd Friday of Feb for $1.40. Your net investment is $1.60 per contract.
>
> If ABC stays at $30 or rises, the ABC Feb 30 put expires worthless. Now, with your net cost of ABC May 30 at $1.60 ($3.00 minus $1.40) you sell a March 30 put for $1.00. Your net cost is now only $0.60. If ABC drops to $28 by Mar expiration you have a $1.00 loss in the March put sold ($2.00 minus $1.00 premium received).
>
> **_Your long put owned_**, May 30 is worth $3.50 ($2.00 intrinsic value + $1.50 time premium) **_since it expires in May and has 2 more months to run_**.
> You now buy back the March 30 for $2.00 + sell an Apr 30 put for $2.50 ($0.50 net credit). If the stock rises to $29 by Apr expiration you buy back the Apr 30 sold for $1.00 and sell your May 30 for $1.75 to cover the trade ($0.75 net credit).
>
> **Recap:** Costs of trade: $1.60 debit. Profits from trade: $2.25 credit.

- ## Why should we sell "Puts" for spreads in this market?

Answers:

1. Because people who buy Puts are primarily short term bearish, and because it is human nature to be optimistic and bullish.

2. People do not wish to take losses in the market. Nobody likes to admit that they made a wrong decision, so if they buy Puts to protect against a decline it will usually be short term. Supply and demand determines option

prices. If the demand is great relative to the supply, the price rises! That translates into overvalued, short-term put prices relative to the longer term.

That is why, it pays to implement calendar spreads, because we are buying longer term undervalue and reducing our cost basis by capturing short-term overvalue and allowing the passage of time to earn us the premium. When we have captured sufficient premium to cover the cost of the long Put, plus any differential in strike prices, we enjoy a FREE RIDE with no investment cost. Does this strategy make sense to you? Of course it does.

In any Bear market there are spike rallies. That is why we offer the free email pager to our yearly Platinum Plan client renewals. Because when the underlying stock rallies, the short-term contracts that we sold must be repurchased. We advise you to nail down 35% plus profits and repurchase 35% + lower than the price of the near term you previously sold. However you should use OPM to buy back the Put by selling the next consecutive month put (for a credit). If you don't follow our strategy, you may lose the trading profit opportunity. You can't go wrong taking repeated 35% + profits. Remember, a larger number will contract more on an absolute basis than a smaller number. Therefore, if you sell a put for 5, vs. allowing a put, selling at 1, to contact to zero at expiration, you definitely have a better chance of making more profit. A two-point rise in the underlying stock may result in the put sold at 5 to drop to 3 ¼, but the put selling at 1 may drop to 5/8, depending on proximity to expiration date.

3. If the stock price continues to decline, the value of the long-term put will increase, but it will hold its time premium relative to the short-term put sold. You should be protected as long as the decline is not precipitous, in which case, both puts will be deeply **In-The-Money (ITM)** and lose their time premium. If that happens, you may repurchase your short-term Put at its intrinsic value, and sell the next consecutive month Put for some small time premium, then wait for a rally to repurchase it for a worthwhile profit.

- **Why should you continue to hold losses in stocks that may not recover to their former levels?**

Consider this alternative strategy!

Suppose you bought CSCO at 50 and it is down to 20 now. You ask: How low can it drop? We don't know the answer, but we do know that there are millions of investors like you who are in the same dilemma. They are all waiting to break even and get out without a loss. Guess what that does to the

stock on a rise. Stock prices are dictated by supply and demand. If lot of overhead supply exists, that puts pressure on halting a stock price rise, so what happens? The stock drifts downward, re-testing former support levels, while you chase it downward in an effort to sell, and cut your losses.

Better alternative:

Sell out your 1000 shares of CSCO while freeing up $20,000.00 of cash. Buy a July 20 Put and simultaneously sell an April 20 Put for a $1,375.00 net investment, plus commissions. You could execute the equivalent of 5,000 shares for $6,875.00, plus commissions. You should have $25,000 available in non-margined securities in case you wish to write Puts at 25 or 27.5 on a sharp rise in the price of CSCO. If CSCO shares remain at $20.00 during the next month, you will have earned the premium of $187.50 per hundred shares (or one contract. Then, you sell May 20 Puts and receive another $ 187.50 per 100 shares. Now, you have recovered $375.00 of the cost of your July 20 Put of $325.00, or you have a net credit of $50, and no margin requirement. You can't lose no matter what happens. If CSCO shares drop to $16.00 by May expiration, you repurchase the May 20 Put at $4.00, and sell June 20 Put for 5 1/8. Your July 20 Put is worth much more with CSCO at $16.00, than $20.00. Suppose the market and CSCO rallies in June. CSCO rises to $24.00. You buy back your June 20 Put when you have 35% profit in the position at $3.32 and sell a June 22.5 Put for $3.00 (more or less depending upon the time to expiration in June). If the stock remains at $24.00 per share, the June 22.5 will be 0. You can then sell a July 25 Put for 1 3/4 (approximately). You can extend your July 20 Put to an October Put very cheaply, since it is 4 points **Out-of-The-Money (OTM)**, and continue the ride.

Compare that with the mitigation of holding your losing CSCO stock, which has rallied 4 points.

Let's continue with the CSCO loss scenario. If you wish to reacquire CSCO stock that you sold at $20.00 per share at a discount, with full downside loss protection, the July 20 vs. April 20 Put strategy will work. Assume that the

CSCO share price drops to $15.00 and the April 20 Put is 5 points in the money, and will be exercised. You sold the Put and received $187.50 premium. You buy the stock at 18 1/8 effectively (20 minus 1 7/8). You sell a May 20 Call and lower your cost basis on the stock by another $100.00. If the stock continues downward, you have the right to sell it at 20 until July. Your new cost basis is 17 1/8. If you wish to continue to hold it, and it falls

to 5, you are completely protected. You have received more premiums, so you will not lose by holding it.

If the stock price rises to $25.00 by May's expiration date, you can repurchase the May 20 Call, previously sold for $100.00, for $500.00, and sell a June 25 Call for (approximately) 3 1/4.

You then have a 3/4 net loss in the call position, but you have made the profit back on the stock to the 28 1/4 level.

Not a bad risk/reward ratio!

- **What is a good alternative to buying stock?**

If you are among the many investors that own stock portfolios that are severely damaged, you should consider the following strategy to mitigate, and possibly recover, your portfolio value. The severe negatives weighing on the market that may push below the previous last year support level of 2150 are bad news from Sun Micro, Motorola, and IBM, etc.

Let's use an example of MACR, presently trading at 25 13/16. If you were holding 100 shares of that stock, and tying up $2,575.00 of capital in the stock, consider the following: Sell the stock out, and implement 10 contracts of the following neutral Put Calendar Spread, with no margin required.

Buy 10 MACR Aug 25 Puts (4 1/2) -- Sell 10 MACR Mar 25 Puts (1 3/4) for a 2 3/4 debit. The total investment is $2,750.00, plus modest commission.

- ## SCENARIO A

(STOCK REMAINS VIRTUALLY UNCHANGED)

If the stock price stays at 25 13/16, or falls to 25, you will earn $1,750.00 income in less than 1 month. Your long position will remain at the same value because it has 5 more months until expiration. At expiration, sell an April 25 Put for $2,000. 00. Now you have recovered $3,750.00 income of the $4,500.00 cost of the August Puts (small risk).

- ## SCENARIO B

(STOCK FALLS TO 20)

If the stock price falls to 20, the April 25 Put will be at 5 on expiration. You will be able to sell May 25 Puts for 6 1/4 and the value of your Aug 25 Puts will have increased substantially, with 3 more consecutive months to recover your initial premium for a positive cash flow. If you had held the stock, you would have sustained a further 5-point loss (which would be terribly depressing).

- ## SCENARIO C

(STOCK RISES TO 30 +)

If the stock price rises to 30, the April Put will expire and you can keep taking profits by selling high and buying back cheaper, as we have been doing in our normal strategies. This is the value of a Put Calendar Spread. Instead of you using your investment funds to repurchase the Put sold, you sell the next consecutive month Put for more time value premium, for a net credit.

You are reducing your risk, and investment, by using **Other-People's-Money (OPM)**, not your money. Of course, you will need margin requirements to support the differential in strike prices between long and shorts, but the risk is controllable.

You may repeat the process over and over again as the stock continues to rise in price. Sell for more premium, then cancel the contact for 35% + less. Is this not a better strategy than investing in more stock, hoping that you've found the elusive bottom? The bottom line in investing is managing your risk. If you can do so using **OPM**, then you become the casino owner emptying the slot machines every night, instead of the casino player trying to hit the jackpot.

Good fortune!

- **Why should we use Puts for spreads in this market?**

Answers:

Because people who buy Puts are primarily short term bearish, because it is human nature to be optimistic and bullish.

People do not wish to take losses in the market. Nobody likes to admit that they made a wrong decision, so if they buy puts to protect against a decline it will usually be short term. Supply and demand determines option prices. If the demand is great relative to the supply, the price rises! That translates into overvalued short term Put prices relative to the longer term. That is why, it pays to implement calendar spreads, because we are buying longer term undervalue and reducing our cost basis by capturing short term overvalue and allowing the passage of time to earn us the premium. When we have captured sufficient premium to cover the cost of the long Put plus any differential in strike prices, we enjoy a FREE RIDE with no investment cost. Does this strategy make sense? Of course it does. In any bear market there are spike rallies. That is why we offer the free email pager to our yearly Platinum Plan client renewals. Because when the underlying stock rallies, the short term Put that we sold contracts, and we advise you to nail down 35% plus profits and repurchase 35% + lower than the price that you sold the near term Put for. However you should use **OPM** to buy back the put by selling the next consecutive month put (for a credit). If you don't follow our strategy, you may loose the trading profit opportunity. You can't go wrong taking repeated 35% + profits. Remember, a larger number of contracts more on an absolute basis than a smaller number. Therefore is you sell a Put for 5 versus allowing a Put selling at 1 to contact to zero at expiration, you definitely have a better chance of making more profit. A 2-point rise in the underlying stock may result the Put sold at 5 to drop to 3 ¼, but the Put selling at 1 may drop to 5/8, depending on proximity to expiration date.

If the stock continues to decline the value of the long term Put will increase, but it will hold its time premium relative to the short term Put sold, and you should be protected, as long as the decline is not precipitous, in which case, both Puts will be deeply in the money and lose their time premium. If that happens, you may repurchase your short Put at its intrinsic value and sell the next consecutive month Put for some small time premium and hope for a rally to repurchase it for a worthwhile profit.

- **If I am "*assigned*" on any In-The-Money (ITM) short Puts, what are my choices?**

Answer:

In dealing with **In-The-Money (ITM) short Put** **assignments** you have 2 choices:

Choice # 1:

1. Keep the stock which you bought at a discount to the extent of the premium received when it was sold.

2. Sell a covered Call on the stock at a strike price just above the present price of the stock.

Choice # 2:

Sell the stock (day trade) and sell the next consecutive month Put at a strike price equal or above the strike price of the long Put owned.

Which method that you choose depends on the size of your portfolio and available capital funds.

- ## How do I calculate profits on option trades?

Profit Calculation:

Do not look at net liquidating value. This does not account for the premium income that you will earn month by month until your long Put expires.

Do consider net credits over net debits for profit to date. If you are assigned on a sold Put your profit or loss = the strike price of the Put sold, less - the stock price presently, add the premium received for the original Put sold, add the premium on the new Put sold vs. the long Put owned.

Appendix 2: Definitions of Terms

<u>Assignment</u> or <u>Exercise of Option Sold</u>

When the option sold has no more time value premium it will be assigned to the broker which means that the stock **must be** bought from the Put holder at the strike price of the option in the case of a Put, **or**, the stock must be delivered to the option holder at the strike price in the case of a Call.

<u>Bear Spreads</u>

Bear spreads are a technique utilized in playing a downward move in a stock. It consists of covered put option writing to minimize your risk and increase your returns. Typically, selling stock short and buying a call option for protection is riskier than bear spreads.

We take option writing to the next level. One of our techniques is bear spreads, which means buying a longer term, relatively undervalued put option at a higher strike price to hedge the overvalued short term put option written at a lower strike price. Bear spreads increase returns while hedging against risk.

When you execute bear spreads and your stock falls, you will enjoy more numerical growth (on an absolute basis) of the long-term Put than the short-term Put. Bear spreads will shrink the premium of the put option written or sold, if it has a near term expiration, and that will inure to your benefit. Bear spreads provide better leverage and less downside than shorting stock.

<u>Bull Spreads</u>

You may have been exposed to the investment technique of option writing. Option writing is a generic term of capturing premiums from option buyers who are willing to put their money on the line to make an anticipated profit on the upward or downward movement of a given stock. Covered call writers buy the underling stock and sell a Call for a premium return capture regardless of the movement of the stock. But if the stock declines by more than the premium collected, the covered call option writer could sustain a loss. However, we take covered call option writing to the next level. Instead of buying stock and selling calls, which is very simplistic, and does not keep the investor totally hedged, we recommend buying a longer term, relatively undervalued option to hedge the overvalued short term option written. This is referred to as bull time spreads. When the stock rises, we will enjoy more numerical growth (on an absolute basis) of the long-term Call than the short-term Call (because it is has a lesser numerical value), particularly if the long term is more **"In-The-Money"** **(ITM)**. Bull spreads will shrink the premium of the option writing Call sold, and that will inure to the benefit of the option writer. Bull Time spreads enjoy better leverage and less downside than covered call writing.

Calendar Spreads

Covered call writers buy the underling stock and sell a Call for a premium return capture regardless of the movement of the stock. But if the stock declines by more than the premium collected, the covered call option writer could sustain a loss. However, we take covered call option writing to the next level. Instead of buying stock and selling Calls, which is very simplistic, and does not keep the investor totally hedged, we recommend buying a longer term, relatively undervalued option to hedge the overvalued short term option written. This is referred to as calendar spreads. Time will shrink the premium of the option writing put or call sold, and that will inure to the benefit of the option writer. Calendar spreads enjoy better leverage and less downside than covered call writing.

Covered Calls

Covered call writers buy the underling stock and sell a Call for a premium return capture regardless of the movement of the stock. But if the stock declines by more than the premium collected, the covered call option writer could sustain a loss. However, we take covered call option writing to the next level. Instead of buying stock and selling Calls, which is very simplistic, and does not keep the investor totally hedged, we recommend buying a longer term, relatively undervalued option to hedge the overvalued short term option written. Time will shrink the premium of the option writing Put or Call sold, and that will inure to the benefit of the option writer. This enjoys better leverage and less downside than covered call writing.

Put Spreads

Put spreads are a technique utilized for several intended results. Put spreads can be bearish, neutral to mildly bullish, or overtly bullish. This depends on the horizontal or vertical orientation of the Puts bought vs. those sold. Consult our case studies page on our website for greater understanding.

A Put is a contract between buyer and seller to deliver stock at a specific predetermined fixed price (striking price) for a fixed period of time (term) in exchange for a premium paid by the buyer to the seller (negotiable). The buyer is bearish, and the seller or writer is bullish. Put prices move inversely with the price of the underlying stock.

Put Option writing is a generic term of capturing premiums from put option buyers who are willing to put their money on the line to make an anticipated profit on the downward movement of a given stock. Covered put writers sell short the underling stock and sell a put for a premium return capture regardless of the movement of the stock. However, we take covered put option writing to the next level. Instead of selling short stock and selling puts, which is very simplistic, and does not keep the investor totally hedged, we recommend buying a longer term, relatively undervalued, put options to hedge the overvalued short term put option written. This is referred to as bull put time spreads. When the stock rises, we will enjoy more numerical shrinkage (on an absolute basis) of the short term Put than the long term Put (because it is has a greater numerical value), particularly if the short term is more **"In-The-Money" (ITM)** or **"At-The-Money" (ATM)**. Put spreads will shrink the premium of the option written or put sold, if the stock remains unchanged or rises, and that will inure to the benefit of the option writer. Bull Put Time spreads enjoy better leverage and less downside than covered call writing.

Risk Management

Risk management is a protective strategy in the stock market. You should always use risk management to hedge your bet in order to be safer. Option writing is a generic term of capturing premiums from option buyers who are willing to put their money on the line to make an anticipated profit on the upward or downward movement of a given stock. Covered call writers buy the underling stock and sell a call for a premium return capture regardless of the movement of the stock. This is a partial risk management. If the stock declines by more than the premium collected, the covered call option writer owns a partial hedge, (some degree of risk management) but could sustain a loss. However, we, being proponents of risk management, take covered call option writing to the next level. Instead of buying stock and selling Calls, which is very simplistic, and does not keep the investor totally hedged, we recommend, buying a longer term, relatively undervalued option to hedge the overvalued short term option written. Time will shrink the premium of the option writing Put or Call sold, and that will insure to the benefit of the option writer affording more risk management. This enjoys a strong hedge, better leverage and less downside than covered call writing.

Appendix 3: Graphs of Common Movements

Reduction in Capital cost of long calls from short call premiums captured

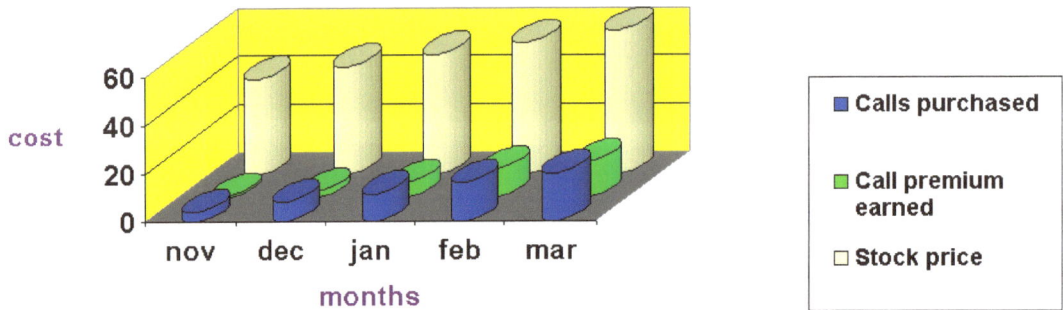

Assumption #1: The stock price rises steadily from 40 to 60 during the five-month period.

Assumption #2: The client repurchases the short Calls sold and rolls up to the next month at a 40 strike price.

Assumption #3: The client purchases a March 40 call and sells a Nov 45 call (Bull calendar call spread).

Reduction in Capital cost of long calls from short call premiums captured

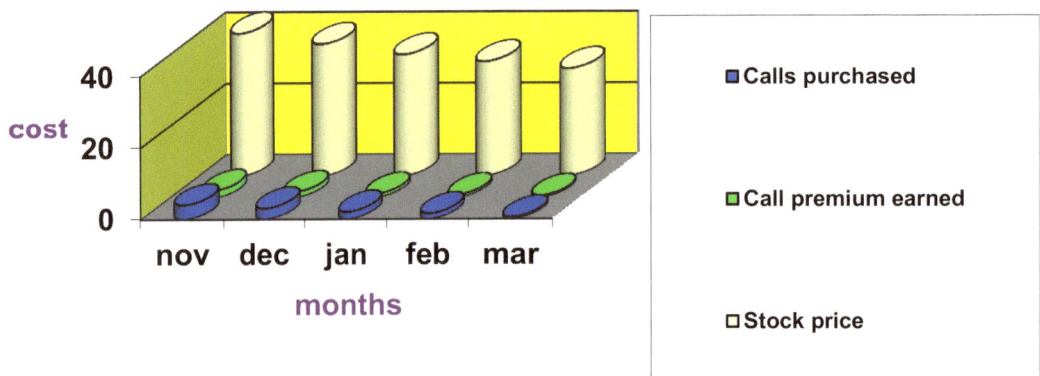

Assumption #1: The stock price falls steadily from 40 to 30 during the five-month period.

Assumption #2: The client repurchases the short Calls sold and rolls out to the next month.

Reduction in Capital cost of long puts from short put premiums captured

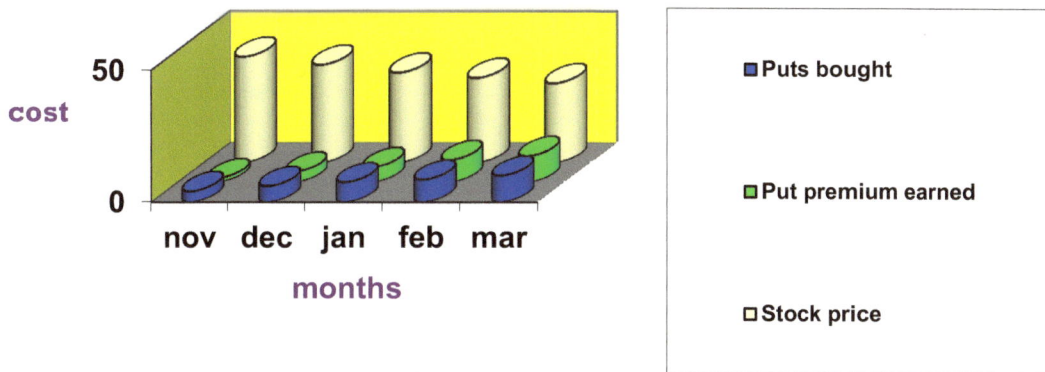

Assumption #1: The stock price falls steadily from 40 to 30 during the five-month period.

Assumption #2: The client repurchases the short Calls sold and rolls out to the next month.

Reduction in Capital cost of long calls from short call premiums captured

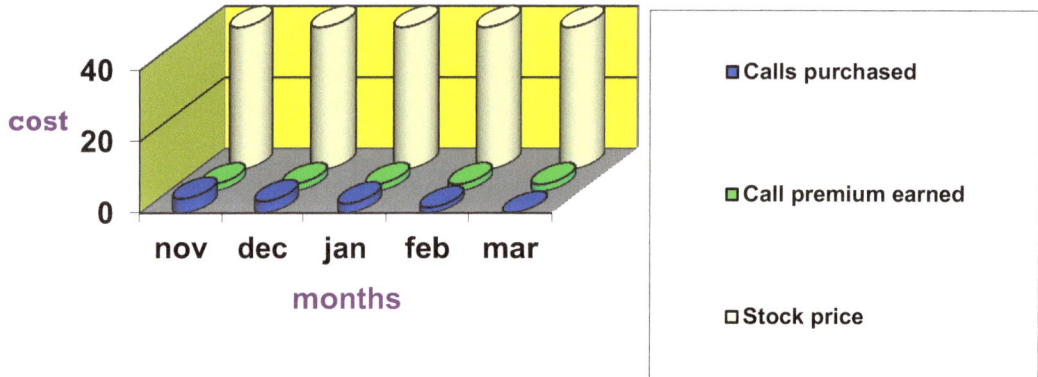

Legend:
- ■ Calls purchased
- ■ Call premium earned
- □ Stock price

(y-axis: cost — 0, 20, 40; x-axis: months — nov, dec, jan, feb, mar)

Assumption #1: The stock price remains unchanged at 40 during the five-month period.

Assumption #2: The client repurchases the short Calls sold and rolls out to the next month at 40 strike price.

Reduction in Capital cost of long options from short option premiums captured

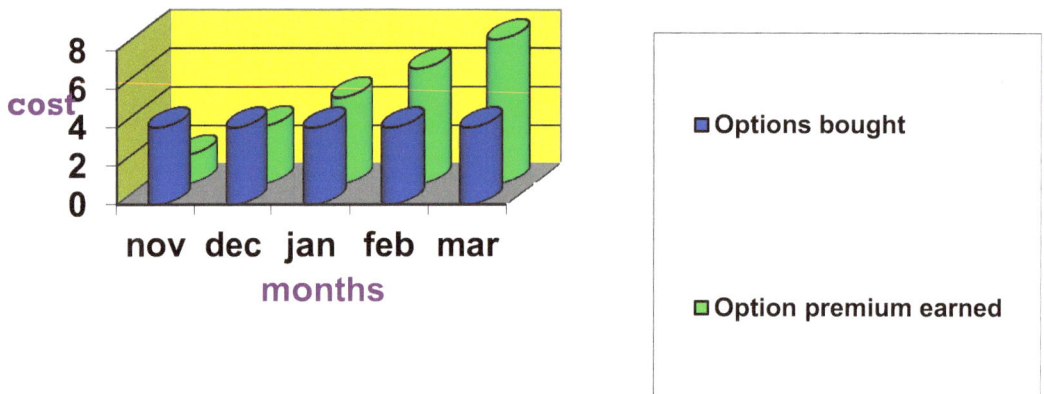

Legend:
- ■ Options bought
- ■ Option premium earned

(y-axis: cost — 0, 2, 4, 6, 8; x-axis: months — nov, dec, jan, feb, mar)

Assumption: The stock price remains unchanged during the five-month period.

Reduction in Capital cost of long calls from short call premiums captured

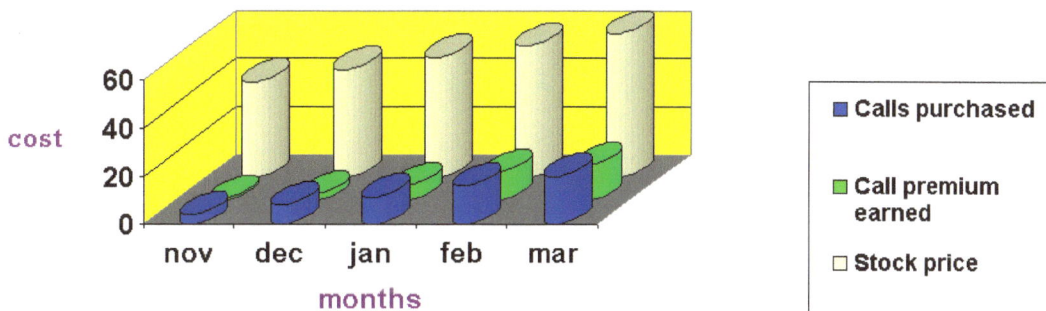

Assumption #1: The stock price rises steadily from 40 to 60 during the five-month period.

Assumption #2: The client repurchases the short Calls sold and rolls up to the next month at a 40 strike price.

* * * * * * * * *

Appendix 4: 2007 Year Track Record

Performance for the Year 2007: Short Put Sells as of December 31, 2007 follows:

STOCK	TRADING INFORMATION	SHORT PUT		PURCHASE PRICE	PURCHASE SHORT SIDE CLOSED	SELL TO CLOSE FOR:	ORIGINAL PURCHASE PRICE	DATE CLOSED	Type of Notice	GAIN / (LOSS)	% RTN SHORT ONLY	$$$$ BASED ON 10 CONTRACTS
AAPL	86.50 + 1.65	Jan	85	$ 4.40	$ 3.30			1/3/2007	Sold, Buyback, Sell	$ 1.10	33%	$ 1,100.00
AAPL	92.23 + 6.76	Feb	85	$ 4.50	$ 2.15			1/9/2007	Sold, Buyback, Sell	$ 2.35	109%	$ 2,350.00
AAPL	95.60 + 3.03	Feb	90	$ 3.90	$ 2.70			1/10/2007	Sold, Buyback, Sell	$ 1.20	44%	$ 1,200.00
AAPL	85.00 + .20	0	0	$ -	$ -			2/13/2007	Roll	$ -		$ -
AAPL	88.37 + 2.47	Mar	90	$ 6.60	$ 3.25			2/21/2007	Sold, Buyback, Sell	$ 3.35	103%	$ 3,350.00
AAPL	89.99 + 2.02	Apr	90	$ 4.50	$ 3.20			3/12/2007	Sold, Buyback, Sell	$ 1.30	41%	$ 1,300.00
AAPL	91.55 + 2.00	Apr	95	$ 6.50	$ 4.95			3/19/2007	Sold, Buyback, Sell	$ 1.55	31%	$ 1,550.00
AAPL	94.60 + 1.08	May	95	$ 6.60	$ 4.90			3/26/2007	Sold, Buyback, Sell	$ 1.70	35%	$ 1,700.00
AAPL	101.33 + 5.95	May	100	$ 8.00	$ 1.90			4/26/2007	Sold, Buyback, Sell	$ 6.10	321%	$ 6,100.00
AAPL	102.90 + 2.09	Jun	100	$ 3.30	$ 1.95			5/7/2007	Sold, Buyback, Sell	$ 1.35	69%	$ 1,350.00
AAPL	108.23 + 1.35	Jun	105	$ 4.15	$ 2.40			5/10/2007	Sold, Buyback, Sell	$ 1.75	73%	$ 1,750.00
AAPL	110.02	Jun	110	$ 4.70	$ 3.20			5/21/2007	Sold, Buyback, Sell	$ 1.50	47%	$ 1,500.00
AAPL	114	Jul	110	$ 5.70	$ 3.80			5/23/2007	Sold, Buyback, Sell	$ 1.90	50%	$ 1,900.00
AAPL	121.19	Jun	115	$ 3.60	$ 0.85			6/1/2007	Sold, Buyback, Sell	$ 2.75	324%	$ 2,750.00
AAPL	126.22 + 2.58	Jul	115	$ 3.00	$ 2.00			6/7/2007	Sold, Buyback, Sell	$ 1.00	50%	$ 1,000.00
AAPL	130.00 + 2.83	Jul	120	$ 3.45	$ 0.70			7/5/2007	Sold, Buyback, Sell	$ 2.75	393%	$ 2,750.00
AAPL	133.29 + 3.24	Aug	120	$ 3.20	$ 2.10			7/10/2007	Sold, Buyback, Sell	$ 1.10	52%	$ 1,100.00
AAPL	139.08 + 1.35	Aug	125	$ 3.50	$ 2.05			7/16/2007	Sold, Buyback, Sell	$ 1.45	71%	$ 1,450.00
AAPL	145.07 + 7.81	Aug	130	$ 3.30	$ 0.90			7/26/2007	Sold, Buyback, Sell	$ 2.40	267%	$ 2,400.00
AAPL	0	0	0	$ -	$ -			7/31/2007	Roll	$ -		$ -
AAPL	142.25 + 3.77	Sep	135	$ 5.50	$ 2.35			9/4/2007	Sold, Buyback, Sell	$ 3.15	134%	$ 3,150.00
AAPL	142.45 + 1.53	Oct	135	$ 5.15	$ 3.05			9/19/2007	Sold, Buyback, Sell	$ 2.10	69%	$ 2,100.00
AAPL	148.25 + 4.10	Oct	140	$ 4.75	$ 2.75			9/24/2007	Sold, Buyback, Sell	$ 2.00	73%	$ 2,000.00
AAPL	164.81 + 2.35	Nov	140	$ 5.85	$ 1.75			10/8/2007	Sold, Buyback, Sell	$ 4.10	234%	$ 4,100.00
AAPL	173.46 + 3.04	Nov	145	$ 2.60	$ 1.68			10/22/2007	Sold, Buyback, Sell	$ 0.92	55%	$ 920.00
AAPL	189.95	Dec	145	$ 3.30	$ 0.30			11/1/2007	Sold, Buyback, Sell	$ 3.00	1000%	$ 3,000.00
AAPL	198.57	Apr	150	$ 3.55	$ 3.55			12/28/2007	Market Letter	$ -		$ -
AAPL	200	0	0	$ -	$ -			12/28/2007	Close	$ -		$ -
ACL	0	0	0	$ -	$ -			6/11/2007	Close	$ -		$ -
ACL	135.00 + 4.93	Nov	125	$ 3.20	$ 3.20			6/29/2007	Market letter			

STOCK	TRADING INFORMATION	SHORT PUT		PURCHASE PRICE	PURCHASE SHORT SIDE CLOSED	SELL TO CLOSE FOR:	ORIGINAL PURCHASE PRICE	DATE CLOSED	Type of Notice	GAIN / (LOSS)	% RTN SHORT ONLY	$$$ BASED ON 10 CONTRACTS
ACL	136.64 + 3.19	Aug	130	$ 0.90	$ 0.55			7/3/2007	Sold, Buyback, Sell	$ 0.35	64%	$ 350.00
ACL	141.09 + 1.42	Aug	130	$ 2.20	$ 1.45			7/11/2007	Sold, Buyback, Sell	$ 0.75	52%	$ 750.00
ACL	145.00 + 2.00	Aug	135	$ 2.50	$ 1.50			7/23/2007	Sold, Buyback, Sell	$ 1.00	67%	$ 1,000.00
ACL	136.93	Jan	130	$ 5.25	$ 5.25			9/7/2007	Market letter			
ACL	147.27	Nov	140	$ 2.60	$ 1.30			10/10/2007	Sold, Buyback, Sell	$ 1.30	100%	$ 1,300.00
ACL	149.13 + 1.36	Nov	145	$ 3.60	$ 2.30			10/26/2007	Sold, Buyback, Sell	$ 1.30	57%	$ 1,300.00
ACL	153.74 + 1.55	Dec	145	$ 4.20	$ 2.60			11/1/2007	Sold, Buyback, Sell	$ 1.60	62%	$ 1,600.00
ACL	145.1	0	0	$ -	$ -			11/12/2007	Close	$ -		$ -
ACL	143.09 - 3.18	0	0	$ -	$ -			12/18/2007	Roll	$ -		$ -
ACL	145.23 + 1.18	Jan	150	$ 8.65	$ 5.90			12/31/2007	Sold, Buyback, Sell	$ 2.75	47%	$ 2,750.00
ADBE	42.00 + .30	0	0	$ -	$ -			5/14/2007	Roll	$ -		$ -
ADBE	42.94 + .56	Jun	43	$ 2.00	$ 1.10			5/29/2007	Sold, Buyback, Sell	$ 0.90	82%	$ 900.00
ADBE	44.11 + 1.38	Jul	43	$ 1.60	$ 1.15			6/13/2007	Sold, Buyback, Sell	$ 0.45	39%	$ 450.00
ADBE	45	Oct	45	$ 2.50	$ 0.70			10/10/2007	Sold, Buyback, Sell	$ 1.80	257%	$ 1,800.00
ADBE	46.52 + .55	Nov	45	$ 1.45	$ 0.70			10/18/2007	Sold, Buyback, Sell	$ 0.75	107%	$ 750.00
ADBE	47.61 + 69	Apr	45	$ 2.65	$ 2.65			11/2/2007	Market letter			
ADBE	42.87	0	0	$ -	$ -			11/12/2007	Roll	$ -		$ -
ADBE	44.08 + .75	Dec	45	$ 3.00	$ 1.80			12/5/2007	Sold, Buyback, Sell	$ 1.20	67%	$ 1,200.00
AGN	58.5	0	0	$ -	$ -			7/16/2007	Miscellaneous	$ -		$ -
AGN	63.96 + 3.17	Jan	60	$ 2.40	$ 2.40			8/2/2007	Market letter			
AGN	65.67 - .31	Oct	60	$ 4.30	$ 0.50			10/16/2007	Sold, Buyback, Sell	$ 3.80	760%	$ 3,800.00
AGN	67.40 + .53	Nov	65	$ 1.85	$ 0.85			11/5/2007	Sold, Buyback, Sell	$ 1.00	118%	$ 1,000.00
AGN	67.30 + .86	Dec	65	$ 1.70	$ 0.60			12/4/2007	Sold, Buyback, Sell	$ 1.10	183%	$ 1,100.00
APA	79.29 + 1.48	Jun	75	$ 1.55	$ 0.55			5/21/2007	Sold, Buyback, Sell	$ 1.00	182%	$ 1,000.00
APA	85.26 + 1.38	Jul	75	$ 1.35	$ 0.25			6/14/2007	Sold, Buyback, Sell	$ 1.10	440%	$ 1,100.00
APA	86.40 + 1.79	Jul	80	$ 0.80	$ 0.45			6/21/2007	Sold, Buyback, Sell	$ 0.35	78%	$ 350.00
APA	85.85 - .34	Jul	85	$ 1.70	$ 0.70			7/16/2007	Sold, Buyback, Sell	$ 1.00	143%	$ 1,000.00
APA	103.72 + 4.54	Apr	90	$ 3.80	$ 3.80			11/2/2007	Market letter			
APA	105.40 + 2.97	Dec	90	$ 1.15	$ 0.75			11/6/2007	Sold, Buyback, Sell	$ 0.40	53%	$ 400.00
APA	104.98 + 5.00	Dec	95	$ 1.65	$ 0.15			12/12/2007	Sold, Buyback, Sell	$ 1.50	1000%	$ 1,500.00
APA	108.35 + 3.32	Jan	95	$ 1.05	$ 0.55			12/21/2007	Sold, Buyback, Sell	$ 0.50	91%	$ 500.00

STOCK	TRADING INFORMATION	SHORT PUT		PURCHASE PRICE	PURCHASE SHORT SIDE CLOSED	SELL TO CLOSE FOR:	ORIGINAL PURCHASE PRICE	DATE CLOSED	Type of Notice	GAIN / (LOSS)	% RTN SHORT ONLY	$$$ BASED ON 10 CONTRACTS
APC	61.53	May	55	$ 2.55	$ 2.55			12/7/2007	Market letter			
APC	63.36 + 1.81	Jan	58	$ 1.10	$ 0.65			12/12/2007	Sold, Buyback, Sell	$ 0.45	69%	$ 450.00
APC	64.44 + 1.15	Jan	60	$ 1.25	$ 0.70			12/20/2007	Sold, Buyback, Sell	$ 0.55	79%	$ 550.00
APC	66.85 + .55	Jan	60	$ 1.25	$ 0.30			12/26/2007	Sold, Buyback, Sell	$ 0.95	317%	$ 950.00
AVY	52.37 + 1.12	Apr	50	$ 3.20	$ 3.20			11/16/2007	Market letter			
AVY	52.13 + 93	Dec	50		$ 0.20			12/12/2007	Sold, Buyback, Sell	$ (0.20)	-100%	$ (200.00)
AZO	132.85 + 1.18	Dec	125	$ 4.70	$ 4.70			5/18/2007	Market letter			
AZO	0	0	0	$ -	$ -			6/5/2007	Roll	$ -		$ -
AZO	133.10 + 1.42	0	0	$ -	$ -			6/11/2007	Close	$ -		$ -
AZO	135.75 + 1.33	Jul	130	$ 2.65	$ 1.35			6/12/2007	Sold, Buyback, Sell	$ 1.30	96%	$ 1,300.00
AZO	139.92 + 2.53	Jul	135	$ 3.00	$ 1.75			6/18/2007	Sold, Buyback, Sell	$ 1.25	71%	$ 1,250.00
AZN	44.20 - .70	0	0	$ -				11/12/2007	Roll	$ -		$ -
AZN	46.48 + 3.25	Apr	45	$ 2.85	$ 2.85			11/23/2007	Market letter			
AZN	44.65	0	0	$ -				12/18/2007	Roll	$ -		$ -
BA	95.13 + 1.57	0	0	$ -				5/15/2007	Close	$ -		$ -
BA	95.25 + .91	Jun	95	$ 2.75	$ 1.80			5/16/2007	Sold, Buyback, Sell	$ 0.95	53%	$ 950.00
BA	99.20 + .90	Jul	95	$ 1.95	$ 1.35			5/29/2007	Sold, Buyback, Sell	$ 0.60	44%	$ 600.00
BA	101	Jul	100	$ 3.35	$ 2.25			6/1/2007	Sold, Buyback, Sell	$ 1.10	49%	$ 1,100.00
BA	101.32 + 2.43	Jul	105	$ 5.00	$ 3.95			7/6/2007	Sold, Buyback, Sell	$ 1.05	27%	$ 1,050.00
BA	93.49 - 1.33	0	0	$ -				10/16/2007	Roll	$ -		$ -
BA	98.05 + 1.06	Nov	100	$ 8.10	$ 3.40			10/30/2007	Sold, Buyback, Sell	$ 4.70	138%	$ 4,700.00
BA	87.00 - .40	0	0	$ -				12/18/2007	Roll	$ -		$ -
BAY/BAYRY.PK	71.19 + .92	May	70	$ 1.30	$ 0.80			5/7/2007	Sold, Buyback, Sell	$ 0.50	63%	$ 500.00
BAY/BAYRY.PK	71.70 + 2.46	Jun	70	$ 1.55	$ 1.10			5/21/2007	Sold, Buyback, Sell	$ 0.45	41%	$ 450.00
BAY/BAYRY.PK	74.21 + 45	Jul	70	$ 1.80	$ 1.10			6/5/2007	Sold, Buyback, Sell	$ 0.70	64%	$ 700.00
BAY/BAYRY.PK	76.21 + 1.18	Jul	75	$ 3.00	$ 1.90			6/19/2007	Sold, Buyback, Sell	$ 1.10	58%	$ 1,100.00
BAY/BAYRY.PK	81.95	0	0	$ -				10/16/2007	Misc	$ -		$ -
BBY	48.29 + 1.48	Dec	48	$ 3.50	$ 3.50			6/1/2007	Market letter			
BBY	49.37 + .29	Jun	48	$ 0.45	$ 0.20			6/4/2007	Sold, Buyback, Sell	$ 0.25	125%	$ 250.00

STOCK	TRADING INFORMATION	SHORT PUT		PURCHASE PRICE	PURCHASE SHORT SIDE CLOSED	SELL TO CLOSE FOR:	ORIGINAL PURCHASE PRICE	DATE CLOSED	Type of Notice	GAIN / (LOSS)	% RTN SHORT ONLY	$$$ BASED ON 10 CONTRACTS
BBY	47.25 + .10	Jul	48	$ 1.05	$ 0.60			7/16/2007	Sold, Buyback, Sell	$ 0.45	75%	$ 450.00
BBY	48.65 - .60	Oct	50	$ 2.55	$ 1.40			10/16/2007	Sold, Buyback, Sell	$ 1.15	82%	$ 1,150.00
BBY	49.37 + .45	Nov	50	$ 2.10	$ 1.50			10/30/2007	Sold, Buyback, Sell	$ 0.60	40%	$ 600.00
BBY	51.63 + .79	Jun	48	$ 2.40	$ 2.40			12/14/2007	Market letter	$ -		$ -
BBY	0	0	0					12/18/2007	Misc	$ -		$ -
BBY	50.42 - .72	Dec	50	$ 2.45	$ 0.50			12/18/2007	Sold, Buyback, Sell	$ 1.95	390%	$ 1,950.00
BBY	50.42 - .72	0	0					12/18/2007	Roll	$ -		$ -
BBY	50.42 - .72	0	0					12/18/2007	Roll	$ -		$ -
BBY	52.34 + .67	Jan	50		$ 0.75			12/21/2007	Sold, Buyback, Sell	$ (0.75)	-100%	$ (750.00)
BCRM	41.18 + 1.16	Nov	38	$ 1.30	$ 0.75			10/15/2007	Sold, Buyback, Sell	$ 0.55	73%	$ 550.00
BCRM	0	0	0					10/15/2007	Roll	$ -		$ -
BCRM	34	0	0					10/26/2007	Roll	$ -		$ -
BDK	93.19 + .98	Jun	90	$ 2.20	$ 1.25			5/9/2007	Sold, Buyback, Sell	$ 0.95	76%	$ 950.00
BDK	95.28 + .36	Jun	95	$ 3.15	$ 1.60			6/5/2007	Sold, Buyback, Sell	$ 1.55	97%	$ 1,550.00
BDK	96.33 + 6.55	Nov	90	$ 3.40	$ 3.40			6/13/2007	Market letter			
BDK	84.27 - .54	Nov	90			$ 8.30	3.40	7/30/2007	Sell to close	$ 4.90	144%	$ 4,900.00
BDK	89.00 + 1.21	0	0					8/15/2007	Roll	$ -		$ -
BDK	0	0	0					7/19/2007	Roll	$ -		$ -
BDK	79.68 - .52	0	0					10/16/2007	Roll	$ -		$ -
BDK	88.22 + 5.22	Nov	90	$ 10.69	$ 3.60			10/25/2007	Sold, Buyback, Sell	$ 7.09	197%	$ 7,090.00
BDK	0	Jan	85	$ 3.80	$ 3.80			10/26/2007	Market letter	$ -		$ -
BDK	83.38 + .36	0	0					11/12/2007	Roll	$ -		$ -
BGG	32.27 + .54	May	30	$ 0.75	$ 0.10			5/9/2007	Sold, Buyback, Sell	$ 0.65	650%	$ 650.00
BGG	32.71 + .16	Jun	30	$ 0.35	$ 0.10			6/4/2007	Sold, Buyback, Sell	$ 0.25	250%	$ 250.00
BIG	34.30 + .78	Jun	35	$ 2.75	$ 1.95			5/29/2007	Sold, Buyback, Sell	$ 0.80	41%	$ 800.00
BOL	69.62	Jun	55	$ 1.65	$ 0.05			6/12/2007	Sold, Buyback, Sell	$ 1.60	3200%	$ 1,600.00
BWA	81.90 + 1.94	Jul	80	$ 3.00	$ 2.30			5/14/2007	Sold, Buyback, Sell	$ 0.70	30%	$ 700.00
BWA	83.61 + 1.54	Jun	85	$ 3.90	$ 3.00			5/17/2007	Sold, Buyback, Sell	$ 0.90	30%	$ 900.00
BWA	84.87 + 1.15	Jul	85	$ 4.10	$ 2.15			6/21/2007	Sold, Buyback, Sell	$ 1.95	91%	$ 1,950.00
BWA	87.34 + 1.4	Aug	85	$ 3.20	$ 2.00			7/2/2007	Sold, Buyback, Sell	$ 1.20	60%	$ 1,200.00

STOCK	TRADING INFORMATION	SHORT PUT		PURCHASE PRICE	PURCHASE SHORT SIDE CLOSED	SELL TO CLOSE FOR:	ORIGINAL PURCHASE PRICE	DATE CLOSED	Type of Notice	GAIN / (LOSS)	%RTN SHORT ONLY	$$$$ BASED ON 10 CONTRACTS
BWA	90.00 + 1.35	Aug	90	$ 4.40	$ 2.85			7/9/2007	Sold, Buyback, Sell	$ 1.55	54%	$ 1,550.00
BWA	see notes		0	$ -	$ -			8/15/2007	Roll	$ -		$ -
BWA	92.49 - 1.49	Oct	90	$ 1.75	$ 0.50			10/16/2007	Sold, Buyback, Sell	$ 1.25	250%	$ 1,250.00
BWA	97.00 + 1.51	Nov	90	$ 2.25	$ 0.70			10/25/2007	Sold, Buyback, Sell	$ 1.55	221%	$ 1,550.00
BWA	101.84 + 3.88	Dec	90	$ 1.75	$ 1.20			10/29/2007	Sold, Buyback, Sell	$ 0.55	46%	$ 550.00
BWA	101.87 + 2.32	Dec	90	$ 1.75	$ 1.00			11/15/2007	Sold, Buyback, Sell	$ 0.75	75%	$ 750.00
BWA	102.52 + 1.42	Dec	95	$ 1.45	$ 0.50			12/11/2007	Sold, Buyback, Sell	$ 0.95	190%	$ 950.00
BWA	102.52 + 1.42	Jan	95	$ 3.10	$ 1.50			12/11/2007	Sold, Buyback, Sell	$ 1.60	107%	$ 1,600.00
BWA	0		0	$ -	$ -			12/21/2007	Misc	$ -		$ -
CAL	see notes		0	$ -	$ -			5/14/2007	Close	$ -		$ -
CAL	8.74		0	$ -	$ -			10/16/2007	Close	$ -		$ -
CC	0		0	$ -	$ -			6/8/2007	Market letter	$ -		$ -
CC	see notes		0	$ -	$ -			7/16/2007	Roll	$ -		$ -
CC	see notes		0	$ -	$ -			8/15/2007	Roll	$ -		$ -
COP	0		0	$ -	$ -			5/15/2007	Close	$ -		$ -
COP	79.22 + 1.47	Nov	70	$ 1.75	$ 1.75			6/15/2007	Market letter	$ -		$ -
COP	80.67 + 1.45	Jul	75	$ 0.65	$ 0.45			6/15/2007	Sold, Buyback, Sell	$ 0.20	44%	$ 200.00
COP	83.85 + 2.81	Aug	75	$ 1.05	$ 0.35			7/9/2007	Sold, Buyback, Sell	$ 0.70	200%	$ 700.00
COP	87.10 + 1.51	Aug	80	$ 1.15	$ 0.70			7/12/2007	Sold, Buyback, Sell	$ 0.45	64%	$ 450.00
COP	88 + 2.41		0	$ -	$ -			7/12/2007	Roll	$ -		$ -
COP	85.04 + .31	Sep	80	$ 3.90	$ 0.05			9/18/2007	Sold, Buyback, Sell	$ 3.85	7700%	$ 3,850.00
COP	85.32 + .99	Oct	80	$ 1.00	$ 0.18			10/9/2007	Sold, Buyback, Sell	$ 0.82	456%	$ 820.00
COP	79.77		0	$ -	$ -			11/14/2007	Roll	$ -		$ -
COP	83.54 + 1.58		0	$ -	$ -			12/18/2007	Close	$ -		$ -
COP	84.64 + 1.27	May	80	$ 4.15	$ 4.15			12/14/2007	Market letter	$ -		$ -
COP	87.77 + 1.08	Jan	85	$ 2.95	$ 1.11			12/24/2007	Sold, Buyback, Sell	$ 1.84	166%	$ 1,840.00
COST	59.95 + 1.47	Jan	60	$ 2.45	$ 2.45			9/14/2007	Market letter	$ -		$ -
COST	62.65 + .81	Oct	60	$ 1.75	$ 1.00			9/19/2007	Sold, Buyback, Sell	$ 0.75	75%	$ 750.00
COST	68.45 + 5.12	Nov	63	$ 2.05	$ 0.50			10/10/2007	Sold, Buyback, Sell	$ 1.55	310%	$ 1,550.00
COST	66.05 + .76	Nov	65	$ 0.95	$ 0.80			11/12/2007	Sold, Buyback, Sell	$ 0.15	19%	$ 150.00
COST	67.13 + 1.07	Dec	65	$ 2.75	$ 2.10			11/15/2007	Sold, Buyback, Sell	$ 0.65	31%	$ 650.00

STOCK	TRADING INFORMATION	SHORT PUT		PURCHASE PRICE	PURCHASE SHORT SIDE CLOSED	SELL TO CLOSE FOR:	ORIGINAL PURCHASE PRICE	DATE CLOSED	Type of Notice	GAIN / (LOSS)	% RTN SHORT ONLY	$$$ BASED ON 10 CONTRACTS
COST	67.40 + .42	Jan	65	$ 2.80	$ 2.10			11/29/2007	Sold, Buyback, Sell	$ 0.70	33%	$ 700.00
COST	69.10 + 2.15	Jan	68	$ 3.10	$ 2.15			12/4/2007	Sold, Buyback, Sell	$ 0.95	44%	$ 950.00
COST	68.45 + .28	Dec	70	$ 2.45	$ 1.65			12/19/2007	Sold, Buyback, Sell	$ 0.80	48%	$ 800.00
COST	70.90 + .88	Jan	70	$ 3.00	$ 1.45			12/24/2007	Sold, Buyback, Sell	$ 1.55	107%	$ 1,550.00
DO	91.31 + 2.57	Jun	90	$ 4.00	$ 2.35			5/17/2007	Sold, Buyback, Sell	$ 1.65	70%	$ 1,650.00
DO	0	0	0	$ -	$ -			5/21/2007	Misc	$ -		$ -
DO	95.90 + 1.35	Jul	90	$ 2.70	$ 1.60			6/4/2007	Sold, Buyback, Sell	$ 1.10	69%	$ 1,100.00
DO	101.40 + 1.11	Jul	95	$ 3.30	$ 1.05			6/19/2007	Sold, Buyback, Sell	$ 2.25	214%	$ 2,250.00
DO	103.37 + 3.49	Aug	95	$ 2.20	$ 1.60			6/21/2007	Sold, Buyback, Sell	$ 0.60	38%	$ 600.00
DO	112.16 + 3.71	Aug	100	$ 3.10	$ 0.75			7/23/2007	Sold, Buyback, Sell	$ 2.35	313%	$ 2,350.00
DO	0	0	0	$ -	$ -			8/16/2007	Roll	$ -		$ -
DO	109.52 + 2.27	Sep	100	$ -	$ 0.20			9/13/2007	Sold, Buyback, Sell	$ (0.20)	-100%	$ (200.00)
DO	0	0	0	$ -	$ -			9/18/2007	Roll	$ -		$ -
DO	117.00 + 3.12	Nov	100	$ 1.45	$ 0.75			10/11/2007	Sold, Buyback, Sell	$ 0.70	93%	$ 700.00
DO	111.53 + 2.72	Dec	100	$ 1.65	$ 1.20			11/20/2007	Sold, Buyback, Sell	$ 0.45	38%	$ 450.00
DO	0	Dec	100	$ 1.65	$ 0.25			12/3/2007	Sold, Buyback, Sell	$ 1.40	560%	$ 1,400.00
DO	122.82 + 4.87	Jan	100	$ 2.60	$ 0.80			12/6/2007	Sold, Buyback, Sell	$ 1.80	225%	$ 1,800.00
DO	127.70 + 2.40	Jan	100	$ 1.30	$ 0.45			12/10/2007	Sold, Buyback, Sell	$ 0.85	189%	$ 850.00
DO	127	Jan	100	$ 2.54	$ 0.25			12/18/2007	Sold, Buyback, Sell	$ 2.29	916%	$ 2,290.00
DLX	40.12 + 2.66	Jan	35	$ 1.45	$ 1.45			7/27/2007	Market letter	$ -		$ -
DLX	35.75 + .10	0	0	$ -	$ -			9/14/2007	Roll	$ -		$ -
DLX	40.13 + 1.04	Nov	35	$ 1.15	$ 0.25			10/26/2007	Sold, Buyback, Sell	$ 0.90	360%	$ 900.00
DVN	79.10 + 1.15	Jun	75	$ 2.10	$ 0.75			5/21/2007	Sold, Buyback, Sell	$ 1.35	180%	$ 1,350.00
DVN	79.50 + 1.44	Jul	75	$ 1.50	$ 1.00			6/13/2007	Sold, Buyback, Sell	$ 0.50	50%	$ 500.00
DVN	83.53 + 1.47	Jul	80	$ 2.75	$ 0.90			6/18/2007	Sold, Buyback, Sell	$ 1.85	206%	$ 1,850.00
DVN	0	0	0	$ -	$ -			9/15/2007	Roll	$ -		$ -
DVN	0	0	0	$ -	$ -			9/17/2007	Roll	$ -		$ -
DVN	89.87 + .78	Oct	85	$ 3.50	$ 0.20			10/16/2007	Sold, Buyback, Sell	$ 3.30	1650%	$ 3,300.00
DVN	91.08 + 1.08	Nov	85	$ 1.55	$ 0.70			10/31/2007	Sold, Buyback, Sell	$ 0.85	121%	$ 850.00
DVN	94.38 + 1.66	Dec	85	$ 2.05	$ 1.40			11/7/2007	Sold, Buyback, Sell	$ 0.65	46%	$ 650.00
DVN	87.41 + .64	0	0	$ -	$ -			12/19/2007	Roll	$ -		$ -

STOCK	TRADING INFORMATION	SHORT PUT		PURCHASE PRICE	PURCHASE SHORT SIDE CLOSED	SELL TO CLOSE FOR:	ORIGINAL PURCHASE PRICE	DATE CLOSED	Type of Notice	GAIN / (LOSS)	% RTN SHORT ONLY	$$$$ BASED ON 10 CONTRACTS
ESLR	8.82 + .34	0	0	$ -	$ -		$ -	6/13/2007	Roll	$ -	-	$ -
ESLR	9.97 - .39	Jul	10	$ 1.20	$ 0.25			7/16/2007	Sold, Buyback, Sell	$ 0.95	380%	$ 950.00
ESLR	8.93 + .03	0	0	$ -	$ -			8/15/2007	Close	$ -	-	$ -
ESLR	15.99 + 2.34	Mar	15	$ 2.60	$ 2.60		2.60	11/9/2007	Market letter			
ESLR	13.55 + .61	Mar	15			$ 3.40	2.60	11/29/2007	Sell to close	$ 0.80	31%	$ 800.00
ESLR	15.38 + 1.10	Dec	15	$ 1.55	$ 0.90			12/10/2007	Sold, Buyback, Sell	$ 0.65	72%	$ 650.00
ESLR	16.91 + 1.80	Jan	15	$ 1.65	$ 1.00			12/14/2007	Sold, Buyback, Sell	$ 0.65	65%	$ 650.00
ESLR	18.00 + 1.45	Jan	18	$ 2.20	$ 1.40			12/26/2007	Sold, Buyback, Sell	$ 0.80	57%	$ 800.00
ESLR	17.44 + .22	Feb	18	$ 2.05	$ 2.10			12/31/2007	Sold, Buyback, Sell	$ (0.05)	-2%	$ (50.00)
ESRX	95.67 + 1.38	May	95	$ 1.55	$ 0.70			5/14/2007	Sold, Buyback, Sell	$ 0.85	121%	$ 850.00
ESRX	100.59 + 2.03	Jun	95	$ 2.10	$ 0.65			5/24/2007	Sold, Buyback, Sell	$ 1.45	223%	$ 1,450.00
ESRX	101.49 + 1.31	Jul	95	$ 1.80	$ 0.85			6/15/2007	Sold, Buyback, Sell	$ 0.95	112%	$ 950.00
ESRX	53.08 + 1.36	Aug	53	$ 1.85	$ 0.70			8/7/2007	Sold, Buyback, Sell	$ 1.15	164%	$ 1,150.00
ESRX	61.40 + 4.03	Nov	55	$ 1.95	$ 0.25			10/25/2007	Sold, Buyback, Sell	$ 1.70	680%	$ 1,700.00
ESRX	64.47 + .50	Nov	55	$ 1.95	$ 0.05			11/2/2007	Sold, Buyback, Sell	$ 1.90	3800%	$ 1,900.00
ESRX	65.00 + 2.25	Dec	60	$ 2.10	$ 0.60			11/27/2007	Sold, Buyback, Sell	$ 1.50	250%	$ 1,500.00
ESRX	68	May	65	$ 4.45	$ 4.45			11/30/2007	Market letter			
ESRX	70.37 + 2.62	Jan	65	$ 1.65	$ 1.10			12/3/2007	Sold, Buyback, Sell	$ 0.55	50%	$ 550.00
ESRX	73.55 + 1.33	Jan	70	$ 2.75	$ 1.55			12/11/2007	Sold, Buyback, Sell	$ 1.20	77%	$ 1,200.00
FRX	56.25 + 4.37	Nov	50	$ 1.60	$ -			5/23/2007	Misc	$ 1.60		$ 1,600.00
FRX	41.02 - .18	Nov	50			$ 9.30	1.60	7/30/2007	Sell to close	$ 7.70	481%	$ 7,700.00
FRX	38.52 - 1.86	0	0	$ -	$ -			10/16/2007	Roll	$ -	-	$ -
FRX	37.34 + .30	0	0	$ -	$ -			11/13/2007	Close	$ -	-	$ -
FRX	0	0	0	$ -	$ -			11/13/2007	Roll	$ -	-	$ -
FRX	36.70 + .65	0	0	$ -	$ -			12/17/2007	Close	$ -	-	$ -
GD	81.27 + .91	0	0	$ -	$ -			5/15/2007	Close	$ -	-	$ -
GD	0	0	0	$ -	$ -			6/8/2007	Market letter			
GD	80	0	0	$ -	-			6/11/2007	Roll	$ -	-	$ -
GD	81.28 + .88	Jul	80	$ 1.65	$ 1.15			6/20/2007	Sold, Buyback, Sell	$ 0.50	43%	$ 500.00
GD	81.39 + .52	Sep	80	$ 1.40	$ 0.40			9/14/2007	Sold, Buyback, Sell	$ 1.00	250%	$ 1,000.00
GD	88.98 + 1.88	Nov	85	$ 2.90	$ 0.75			10/24/2007	Sold, Buyback, Sell	$ 2.15	287%	$ 2,150.00

STOCK	TRADING INFORMATION	SHORT PUT		PURCHASE PRICE	PURCHASE SHORT SIDE CLOSED	SELL TO CLOSE FOR:	ORIGINAL PURCHASE PRICE	DATE CLOSED	Type of Notice	GAIN/(LOSS)	% RTN SHORT ONLY	$$$ BASED ON 10 CONTRACTS
GD	91.58 + 1.53	Dec	85	$ 1.80	$ 1.15			11/5/2007	Sold, Buyback, Sell	$ 0.65	57%	$ 650.00
GD	93.62 + 1.25	Dec	90	$ 2.60	$ 0.60			12/6/2007	Sold, Buyback, Sell	$ 2.00	333%	$ 2,000.00
GD	88.27 - .05	0	0	$ -	$ -			12/19/2007	Roll	$ -		$ -
GIS	60.00 + .34	May	60	$ 1.09	$ 0.35			5/14/2007	Sold, Buyback, Sell	$ 0.74	211%	$ 740.00
GIS	59.53 + .33	0	0	$ -	-			6/11/2007	Roll	$ -		$ -
GIS	58.68	0	0	$ -	-			7/17/2007	Close	$ -		$ -
GOOG	506.95 + 6.55	Sep	460	$ 9.20	$ 9.20			6/4/2007	Market letter	$ -		$ -
GOOG	552.99	Jul	470	$ 6.30	0.10			7/17/2007	Sold, Buyback, Sell	$ 6.20	6200%	$ 6,200.00
GOOG	503.67 - 4.93	0	0	$ -	-			8/15/2007	Roll	$ -		$ -
GOOG	528.33	Sep	470	$ 5.20	0.05			9/18/2007	Sold, Buyback, Sell	$ 5.15	10300%	$ 5,150.00
GPRO	51	0	0	$ -	-			5/16/2007	Close	$ -		$ -
GPRO	54.09 + 1.10	Nov	50	$ 1.75	1.75			6/1/2007	Market letter	$ -		$ -
GPRO	55.61 + 1.06	Jul	55	$ 2.25	1.20			6/5/2007	Sold, Buyback, Sell	$ 1.05	88%	$ 1,050.00
GPRO	58.50 + 2.69	Aug	55	$ 2.10	1.20			6/26/2007	Sold, Buyback, Sell	$ 0.90	75%	$ 900.00
GPRO	61.38 + 1.4	Aug	60	$ 3.25	1.90			7/13/2007	Sold, Buyback, Sell	$ 1.35	71%	$ 1,350.00
GPRO	63.60 + 1.35	Aug	60	$ 3.25	1.15			7/27/2007	Sold, Buyback, Sell	$ 2.10	183%	$ 2,100.00
GPRO	65.00 + 4.15	Sep	65	$ 1.85	1.20			8/2/2007	Sold, Buyback, Sell	$ 0.65	54%	$ 650.00
GPRO	64.1	0	0	$ -	-			9/17/2007	Roll	$ -		$ -
GPRO	69.69	Nov	65	$ 1.55	1.00			10/11/2007	Sold, Buyback, Sell	$ 0.55	55%	$ 550.00
GPRO	69.45 + 1.90	Nov	70	$ 2.60	1.95			10/31/2007	Sold, Buyback, Sell	$ 0.65	33%	$ 650.00
GPRO	67.33 + 2.60	0	0	$ -	-			11/29/2007	Roll	$ -		$ -
GRMN	59.80 + 1.46	Jun	60	$ 3.00	1.60			5/23/2007	Sold, Buyback, Sell	$ 1.40	88%	$ 1,400.00
GRMN	64.98 + 4.52	Jul	60	$ 2.60	1.05			5/30/2007	Sold, Buyback, Sell	$ 1.55	148%	$ 1,550.00
GRMN	65.32 + 1.5	Jun	65	$ 1.70	0.85			6/11/2007	Sold, Buyback, Sell	$ 0.85	100%	$ 850.00
GRMN	69.06 + 1.63	Jul	65	$ 2.45	1.15			6/14/2007	Sold, Buyback, Sell	$ 1.30	113%	$ 1,300.00
GRMN	72.15 + 1.32	Jul	70	$ 3.20	1.40			6/25/2007	Sold, Buyback, Sell	$ 1.80	129%	$ 1,800.00
GRMN	78.75 + 1.14	Aug	75	$ 3.75	2.75			7/6/2007	Sold, Buyback, Sell	$ 1.00	36%	$ 1,000.00
GRMN	80.35 + .66	Jul	80	$ 2.45	1.45			7/12/2007	Sold, Buyback, Sell	$ 1.00	69%	$ 1,000.00
GRMN	83.21 + .93	Aug	80	$ 4.00	2.95			7/16/2007	Sold, Buyback, Sell	$ 1.05	36%	$ 1,050.00
GRMN	85.71 + 1.35	Aug	85	$ 5.30	3.90			7/26/2007	Sold, Buyback, Sell	$ 1.40	36%	$ 1,400.00
GRMN	92.79 + 8.97	Sep	85	$ 5.30	3.40			8/1/2007	Sold, Buyback, Sell	$ 1.90	56%	$ 1,900.00

STOCK	TRADING INFORMATION	SHORT PUT		PURCHASE PRICE	PURCHASE SHORT SIDE CLOSED	SELL TO CLOSE FOR:	ORIGINAL PURCHASE PRICE	DATE CLOSED	Type of Notice	GAIN / (LOSS)	% RTN SHORT ONLY	$$$$ BASED ON 10 CONTRACTS
GRMN	99.09 + 2.27	Oct	85	$ 4.30	$ 3.00			8/7/2007	Sold, Buyback, Sell	$ 1.30	43%	$ 1,300.00
GRMN	102.13 + 4.41	Sep	90	$ 3.00	$ 1.95			8/21/2007	Sold, Buyback, Sell	$ 1.05	54%	$ 1,050.00
GRMN	114.94 + 4.60	Nov	105	$ 5.00	$ 4.00			10/22/2007	Sold, Buyback, Sell	$ 1.00	25%	$ 1,000.00
GRMN	120.53 + 5.25	Nov	100	$ 2.70	$ 1.55			10/23/2007	Sold, Buyback, Sell	$ 1.15	74%	$ 1,150.00
GRMN	91.68 + 2.33	Jan	95			$ 12.80	$ 3.60	11/8/2007	Sell to close	$ 9.20	256%	$ 9,200.00
GRMN	112.00 + 2.75	Dec	105	$ 6.20	$ 1.60			12/10/2007	Sold, Buyback, Sell	$ 4.60	288%	$ 4,600.00
GRMN	92.34 - 9.52	Dec	95	$ 4.40	-			12/18/2007	Misc	$ 4.40		$ 4,400.00
GRMN	99.50 + 2.54		0	$ -	-			12/20/2007	Roll	$ -		$ -
GSF	68.63 + 1.93	Jun	65	$ 2.55	$ 1.00			5/18/2007	Sold, Buyback, Sell	$ 1.55	155%	$ 1,550.00
GSF	69.42 + 2.12	Jul	65	$ 1.95	$ 1.10			6/13/2007	Sold, Buyback, Sell	$ 0.85	77%	$ 850.00
GSF	79.94 + 5.2	Aug	75	$ 3.66	$ 0.90			7/23/2007	Sold, Buyback, Sell	$ 2.76	307%	$ 2,760.00
GSF	67.00 - .29		0	$ -	-			8/15/2007	Roll	$ -		$ -
GSF	68.70 + 1.55	Sep	70	$ 4.80	$ 3.00			8/23/2007	Sold, Buyback, Sell	$ 1.80	60%	$ 1,800.00
GSF	77.80 + .43	Oct	75	$ 2.00	$ 0.20			10/17/2007	Sold, Buyback, Sell	$ 1.80	900%	$ 1,800.00
GSF	77.80 + .43	Oct	70	$ 4.05	$ 0.05			10/17/2007	Sold, Buyback, Sell	$ 4.00	8000%	$ 4,000.00
GSF	80.00 + .73	Nov	75	$ 1.80	$ 0.75			10/29/2007	Sold, Buyback, Sell	$ 1.05	140%	$ 1,050.00
GSF	85.05 + 1.10	Dec	80	$ 3.55	$ 2.15			11/6/2007	Sold, Buyback, Sell	$ 1.40	65%	$ 1,400.00
GSF	89.00 + 3.12	Dec	85	$ 3.90	$ 2.00			11/26/2007	Sold, Buyback, Sell	$ 1.90	95%	$ 1,900.00
RIG (GSF)	0		0	$ -	-			11/27/2007	Misc	$ -		$ -
RIG (GSF)	134.16		0	$ -	-			12/19/2007	Roll	$ -		$ -
GT	35.30 + .86	Jun	35	$ 2.00	$ 0.85			5/29/2007	Sold, Buyback, Sell	$ 1.15	135%	$ 1,150.00
GT	35.68		0	$ -	-			7/17/2007	Close	$ -		$ -
HAL	38.00 + 1.45	Dec	38	$ 1.45	$ 0.50			12/10/2007	Sold, Buyback, Sell	$ 0.95	190%	$ 950.00
HOG	60.79	Nov	60	$ 3.30	$ 3.30			6/15/2007	Market letter			
HOG	62.77 + 2.53	Jul	60	$ 1.45	$ 0.70			6/22/2007	Sold, Buyback, Sell	$ 0.75	107%	$ 750.00
HOG	56.59 + .19	Nov	60			$ 5.00	3.30	7/30/2007	Sell to close	$ 1.70	52%	$ 1,700.00
HOG	49.20 + 1.08	Feb	48	$ 2.75	$ 2.75			11/9/2007	Market letter			
HOG	49.30 + 1.05	Nov	50	$ 1.40	$ 1.10			11/13/2007	Sold, Buyback, Sell	$ 0.30	27%	$ 300.00
HOG	46.33 + 1.44		0	$ -	-			12/17/2007	Roll	$ -		$ -
IBM	109.20 + .57	Jul	105	$ 0.70	$ 0.45			7/11/2007	Sold, Buyback, Sell	$ 0.25	56%	$ 250.00
IBM	115.79 + .98	Aug	105	$ 1.35	$ 0.20			7/23/2007	Sold, Buyback, Sell	$ 1.15	575%	$ 1,150.00

STOCK	TRADING INFORMATION	SHORT PUT		PURCHASE PRICE	PURCHASE SHORT SIDE CLOSED	SELL TO CLOSE FOR:	ORIGINAL PURCHASE PRICE	DATE CLOSED	Type of Notice	GAIN / (LOSS)	% RTN SHORT ONLY	$$$$ BASED ON 10 CONTRACTS
IBM	114.64 + 2.7	Sep	110	$ 1.40	0.95			8/29/2007	Sold, Buyback, Sell	$ 0.45	47%	$ 450.00
IBM	116.80 - 2.80	Oct	115	$ 2.55	0.40			10/17/2007	Sold, Buyback, Sell	$ 2.15	538%	$ 2,150.00
IBM	100.09 - 6.02	Jan	110			$ 11.60	2.65	11/9/2007	Sell to close	$ 8.95	338%	$ 8,950.00
IBM	101.88 + 1.62	0	0	$ -	-			11/12/2007	Roll	$ -		$ -
IBM	107.42 + 1.61	Dec	110	$ 9.50	4.10			12/4/2007	Sold, Buyback, Sell	$ 5.40	132%	$ 5,400.00
IBM	108.84	Apr	105	$ 4.85	4.85			12/21/2007	Market Letter			
IBM	110.99 + 2.13	Jan	105	$ 1.80	1.30			12/21/2007	Sold, Buyback, Sell	$ 0.50	38%	$ 500.00
IRF	37.39 + 2.39	Dec	35	$ 2.20	2.20			6/22/2007	Market letter			
IRF	38.20 + .27	Jul	40	$ 4.00	2.45			7/3/2007	Sold, Buyback, Sell	$ 1.55	63%	$ 1,550.00
IRF	38.16 + 1.33	Aug	40	$ 3.05	2.10			8/8/2007	Sold, Buyback, Sell	$ 0.95	45%	$ 950.00
IRF	38.34 + .90	Sep	40	$ 2.75	2.25			8/21/2007	Sold, Buyback, Sell	$ 0.50	22%	$ 500.00
IRF	35	0	0	$ -	-			10/17/2007	Roll	$ -		$ -
IRF	36.15 + 2.77	Nov	35	$ 2.45	0.75			11/7/2007	Sold, Buyback, Sell	$ 1.70	227%	$ 1,700.00
IVGN	71.53 + 1.75	Jun	70	$ 2.35	1.35			5/11/2007	Sold, Buyback, Sell	$ 1.00	74%	$ 1,000.00
IVGN	73.77 + 1.02	Jun	75	$ 4.10	2.40			5/23/2007	Sold, Buyback, Sell	$ 1.70	71%	$ 1,700.00
IVGN	74.16 + .20	Jul	75	$ 3.20	2.00			6/20/2007	Sold, Buyback, Sell	$ 1.20	60%	$ 1,200.00
IVGN	75.40 + 1.35	Aug	75	$ 3.10	2.25			7/10/2007	Sold, Buyback, Sell	$ 0.85	38%	$ 850.00
IVGN	77.56 + 8.50	Aug	80	$ 5.40	2.30			8/2/2007	Sold, Buyback, Sell	$ 3.10	135%	$ 3,100.00
IVGN	79.97 + .71	Sep	80	$ 4.10	2.80			8/4/2007	Sold, Buyback, Sell	$ 1.30	46%	$ 1,300.00
IVGN	80.68	Sep	75	$ 3.90	0.05			9/18/2007	Sold, Buyback, Sell	$ 3.85	7700%	$ 3,850.00
IVGN	87.07 + 4.00	Nov	80	$ 1.65	0.20			10/31/2007	Sold, Buyback, Sell	$ 1.45	725%	$ 1,450.00
IVGN	90.70 + 2.30	Dec	85	$ 2.10	0.85			11/14/2007	Sold, Buyback, Sell	$ 1.25	147%	$ 1,250.00
IVGN	91.66 + 1.24	Dec	90	$ 2.40	1.80			11/19/2007	Sold, Buyback, Sell	$ 0.60	33%	$ 600.00
IVGN	94.15 + 2.57	Dec	90	$ 2.40	1.25			11/26/2007	Sold, Buyback, Sell	$ 1.15	92%	$ 1,150.00
IVGN	93.65 + 1.64	Jan	90	$ 2.10	1.75			12/18/2007	Sold, Buyback, Sell	$ 0.35	20%	$ 350.00
KFT	34.12 + .30	Jun	35	$ 2.15	1.35			6/1/2007	Sold, Buyback, Sell	$ 0.80	59%	$ 800.00
KFT	36.24 + 2.28	Dec	35	$ 1.30	1.30			6/22/2007	Market letter			
KFT	36.14 - .60	Jul	35	$ 1.70	0.40			6/22/2007	Sold, Buyback, Sell	$ 1.30	325%	$ 1,300.00
KFT	34.01	0	0	$ -	-			9/18/2007	Roll	$ -		$ -
KFT	34	0	0	$ -	-			9/18/2007	Close	$ -		$ -
KFT	33.95 + .36	Oct	35	$ 1.25	1.05			10/17/2007	Sold, Buyback, Sell	$ 0.20	19%	$ 200.00

STOCK	TRADING INFORMATION	SHORT PUT		PURCHASE PRICE	PURCHASE SHORT SIDE CLOSED	SELL TO CLOSE FOR:	ORIGINAL PURCHASE PRICE	DATE CLOSED	Type of Notice	GAIN / (LOSS)	% RTN SHORT ONLY	$$$ BASED ON 10 CONTRACTS
LLL	95	Jun	95	$ 2.90	$ 0.95			6/12/2007	Sold, Buyback, Sell	$ 1.95	205%	$ 1,950.00
LLL	98.97 + 2.32	Jul	95	$ 2.50	$ 1.10			6/14/2007	Sold, Buyback, Sell	$ 1.40	127%	$ 1,400.00
LLL	99.87	0	0	$ -	$ -			7/17/2007	Close	$ -		$ -
LLL	107.00 + 1.96	Nov	100	$ 1.95	$ 1.10			10/17/2007	Sold, Buyback, Sell	$ 0.85	77%	$ 850.00
LLL	108.00 + 1.00	Nov	105	$ 2.60	$ 0.90			10/30/2007	Sold, Buyback, Sell	$ 1.70	189%	$ 1,700.00
LLL	113.40 + 2.82	Dec	105	$ 2.15	$ 1.15			11/8/2007	Sold, Buyback, Sell	$ 1.00	87%	$ 1,000.00
LLL	112.62 + 1.97	Dec	110	$ 2.35	$ 1.40			12/3/2007	Sold, Buyback, Sell	$ 0.95	68%	$ 950.00
LMT	99.90 + 67	May	100	$ 5.50	$ 0.80			5/15/2007	Sold, Buyback, Sell	$ 4.70	588%	$ 4,700.00
LMT	95	0	0	$ -	$ -			6/13/2007	Roll	$ -		$ -
LMT	103.35 + 3.83	0	0	$ -	$ -			7/24/2007	Bonus	$ -		$ -
LMT	101.38 + 1.36	Sep	100	$ 3.00	$ 1.95			8/27/2007	Sold, Buyback, Sell	$ 1.05	54%	$ 1,050.00
LMT	0	Nov	100	$ 1.50	$ 1.00			10/4/2007	Sold, Buyback, Sell	$ 0.50	50%	$ 500.00
LMT	111.00 + 1.07	Nov	105	$ 2.25	$ 1.45			10/18/2007	Sold, Buyback, Sell	$ 0.80	55%	$ 800.00
LMT	112.50 + .59	Dec	110	$ 4.55	$ 3.00			11/15/2007	Sold, Buyback, Sell	$ 1.55	52%	$ 1,550.00
LMT	110.48	Jan	110	$ 4.15	$ 2.70			12/24/2007	Sold, Buyback, Sell	$ 1.45	54%	$ 1,450.00
LVS	85.11 + 2.69	Aug	80	$ 3.20	$ 1.60			7/25/2007	Sold, Buyback, Sell	$ 1.60	100%	$ 1,600.00
LVS	88.92 + 2.59	Sep	80	$ 2.95	$ 1.80			7/31/2007	Sold, Buyback, Sell	$ 1.15	64%	$ 1,150.00
LVS	98.97 + 4.66	Sep	90	$ 3.75	$ 2.75			8/3/2007	Sold, Buyback, Sell	$ 1.00	36%	$ 1,000.00
LVS	101.00 + 3.43	Sep	95	$ 4.50	$ 2.25			8/29/2007	Sold, Buyback, Sell	$ 2.25	100%	$ 2,250.00
LVS	115.13 + 6.28	Oct	95	$ 4.35	$ 1.10			9/12/2007	Sold, Buyback, Sell	$ 3.25	295%	$ 3,250.00
MGM	82.80 + 1.86	Jan	80	$ 5.60	$ 5.60			8/24/2007	Market letter	$ -		
MGM	83.57 + .39	Sep	80	$ 1.50	$ 0.75			9/6/2007	Sold, Buyback, Sell	$ 0.75	100%	$ 750.00
MGM	86.65 + .90	Oct	80	$ 2.05	$ 1.20			9/19/2007	Sold, Buyback, Sell	$ 0.85	71%	$ 850.00
MGM	99.07 + .78	Nov	85	$ 3.70	$ 1.00			10/9/2007	Sold, Buyback, Sell	$ 2.70	270%	$ 2,700.00
MGM	88.20 + 1.60	0	0	$ -	$ -			11/13/2007	Roll	$ -		$ -
MGM	81.95	0	0	$ -	$ -			12/19/2007	Roll	$ -		$ -
MGM	86.04 + 1.79	Jan	85	$ 6.25	$ 2.45			12/28/2007	Sold, Buyback, Sell	$ 3.80	155%	$ 3,800.00
MKE	63.75	0	0	$ -	$ -			12/18/2007	Roll	$ -		$ -
MRO	105.42 + 1.02	May	105	$ 4.25	$ 1.75			5/8/2007	Sold, Buyback, Sell	$ 2.50	143%	$ 2,500.00
MRO	108.28 + 1.35	Jun	105	$ 3.25	$ 2.00			5/14/2007	Sold, Buyback, Sell	$ 1.25	63%	$ 1,250.00
MRO	112.53 + .77	Jul	105	$ 3.10	$ 2.00			5/17/2007	Sold, Buyback, Sell	$ 1.10	55%	$ 1,100.00

STOCK	TRADING INFORMATION	SHORT PUT		PURCHASE PRICE	PURCHASE SHORT SIDE CLOSED	SELL TO CLOSE FOR:	ORIGINAL PURCHASE PRICE	DATE CLOSED	Type of Notice	GAIN / (LOSS)	% RTN SHORT ONLY	$$$$ BASED ON 10 CONTRACTS
MRO	119.28 + 1.38	Jul	110	$ 3.50	$ 1.55			5/24/2007	Sold, Buyback, Sell	$ 1.95	126%	$ 1,950.00
MRO	63.2	0	0	$ 0	$ -			7/17/2007	Roll	$ -		$ -
MRO	59.25	0	0	$ 0	$ -			10/17/2007	Close	$ -		$ -
MRO	59.44	Jan	58	$ 3.55	$ 3.55			10/19/2007	Market letter			
MRO	62.00 + 2.36	Nov	60	$ 3.00	$ 1.70			10/26/2007	Sold, Buyback, Sell	$ 1.30	76%	$ 1,300.00
MRO	58.80 + 1.14	Dec	60		$ 2.00			12/18/2007	Sold, Buyback, Sell	$ (2.00)	-100%	$ (2,000.00)
MRO	61.10 + 1.26	Jan	60		$ 1.65			12/21/2007	Sold, Buyback, Sell	$ (1.65)	-100%	$ (1,650.00)
NOC	79.23 + 1.93	Jan	75	$ 2.50	$ 2.50			8/2/2007	Market letter			
NOC	80.59 + .30	Oct	80	$ 2.25	$ 0.25			10/17/2007	Sold, Buyback, Sell	$ 2.00	300%	$ 2,000.00
NOC	81.25 + 1.64	Nov	80	$ 1.60	$ 1.20			10/24/2007	Sold, Buyback, Sell	$ 0.40	33%	$ 400.00
NOC	80.00 + 1.21	Dec	80	$ 2.50	$ 1.50			12/3/2007	Sold, Buyback, Sell	$ 1.00	67%	$ 1,000.00
NKE	54.37 + .72 (split 2:1)	May	105	$ 2.05	$ 0.40			4/16/2007	Sold, Buyback, Sell	$ 1.65	413%	$ 1,650.00
NKE	53.16 + .29	0	0	$ -	$ -			5/15/2007	Roll	$ -		$ -
NKE	57.00 + 3.23	Jul	55	$ 3.10	$ 0.40			6/27/2007	Sold, Buyback, Sell	$ 2.70	675%	$ 2,700.00
NKE	59.17 + .88	Aug	60	$ 3.35	$ 1.95			7/2/2007	Sold, Buyback, Sell	$ 1.40	72%	$ 1,400.00
NKE	62.37 + .59	Oct	63	$ 4.20	$ 1.10			10/10/2007	Sold, Buyback, Sell	$ 3.10	282%	$ 3,100.00
NKE	64.19 + 1.04	Nov	60	$ 2.65	$ 0.60			10/15/2007	Sold, Buyback, Sell	$ 2.05	342%	$ 2,050.00
NKE	65.47 + .80	Nov	65	$ 2.20	$ 1.35			10/29/2007	Sold, Buyback, Sell	$ 0.85	63%	$ 850.00
NKE	66.49 + 2.69	Jan	65	$ 2.50	$ 1.40			12/20/2007	Sold, Buyback, Sell	$ 1.10	79%	$ 1,100.00
NOK	26.11 + 1.04	Jun	25	$ 0.85	$ 0.20			5/14/2007	Sold, Buyback, Sell	$ 0.65	325%	$ 650.00
NOK	28.52 + .33	Jul	25	$ 0.45	$ 0.10			6/4/2007	Sold, Buyback, Sell	$ 0.35	350%	$ 350.00
NOK	29.00 + .32	Jul	30	$ 1.75	$ 1.25			7/6/2007	Sold, Buyback, Sell	$ 0.50	40%	$ 500.00
NOK	30.71 + 2.3	Aug	30	$ 2.30	$ 0.30			8/2/2007	Sold, Buyback, Sell	$ 2.00	667%	$ 2,000.00
NOK	31.45 + 1.44	Sep	30	$ 0.90	$ 0.40			8/29/2007	Sold, Buyback, Sell	$ 0.50	125%	$ 500.00
NOK	34.42 + .8	Oct	30	$ 0.90	$ 0.40			9/17/2007	Sold, Buyback, Sell	$ 0.50	125%	$ 500.00
NOK	38.00 + 1.30	Oct	40	$ 3.90	$ 2.35			10/11/2007	Sold, Buyback, Sell	$ 1.55	66%	$ 1,550.00
NOK	36.04 + .73	0	0	$ -	$ -			10/17/2007	Close	$ -		$ -
NOK	39.05 + .08	Nov	35	$ 0.70	$ 0.10			11/2/2007	Sold, Buyback, Sell	$ 0.60	600%	$ 600.00
NOK		Apr	35	$ 2.15	$ 2.15			10/12/2007	Market letter			
NOK	41.80 + .70	Dec	40	$ 2.20	$ 1.05			11/7/2007	Sold, Buyback, Sell	$ 1.15	110%	$ 1,150.00
NOK	40.09 + .60	0	0	$ -	$ -			12/10/2007	Roll	$ -		$ -
NOK	39.38 + .54	Jan	40	$ 2.10	$ 1.55			12/27/2007	Sold, Buyback, Sell	$ 0.55	35%	$ 550.00

STOCK	TRADING INFORMATION	SHORT PUT		PURCHASE PRICE	PURCHASE SHORT SIDE CLOSED	SELL TO CLOSE FOR:	ORIGINAL PURCHASE PRICE	DATE CLOSED	Type of Notice	GAIN / (LOSS)	% RTN SHORT ONLY	$$$ BASED ON 10 CONTRACTS
NOK	38.7	Jul	35	$ 2.35	$ 2.35			12/28/2007	Market letter			
NSM	29.41 + 3.62	Jun	30	$ 3.10	$ 0.95			6/8/2007	Sold, Buyback, Sell	$ 2.15	226%	$ 2,150.00
NSM	29.05	Jul	30	$ 1.35	$ 1.10			7/17/2007	Sold, Buyback, Sell	$ 0.25	23%	$ 250.00
NSM	25.11 + 60	Jan	25	$ 2.35	$ 2.35			8/16/2007	Market letter			
NSM	24.57 + .08	0	0	$ -	$ -			8/16/2007	Close	$ -	-	$ -
NSM	25	0	0	$ -	$ -			10/26/2007	Roll	$ -	-	$ -
NSM	23.17 + .21	0	0	$ -	$ -			11/13/2007	Roll	$ -	-	$ -
NSM	23.12	0	0	$ -	$ -			12/18/2007	Close	$ -	-	$ -
OI	40.05 + 5.01	Jan	35	$ 1.50	$ 1.50			7/27/2007	Market letter			
OI	41.39 + 1.41	Aug	40	$ 1.30	$ 0.60			8/1/2007	Sold, Buyback, Sell	$ 0.70	117%	$ 700.00
OI	40.50 + .85	Sep	40	$ 1.45	$ 1.10			9/5/2007	Sold, Buyback, Sell	$ 0.35	32%	$ 350.00
OI	41.50 + 1.11	Oct	40	$ 1.75	$ 1.05			9/18/2007	Sold, Buyback, Sell	$ 0.70	67%	$ 700.00
OI	45.49 + 1.21	Nov	45	$ 2.75	$ 0.75			11/2/2007	Sold, Buyback, Sell	$ 2.00	267%	$ 2,000.00
OI	45.87 + .98	Dec	45	$ 1.80	$ 0.85			12/3/2007	Sold, Buyback, Sell	$ 0.95	112%	$ 950.00
OI	47.69 + .76	Jan	45	$ 1.65	$ 0.95			12/6/2007	Sold, Buyback, Sell	$ 0.70	74%	$ 700.00
OI	49.13 + .89	Jan	45	$ 1.65	$ 0.60			12/10/2007	Sold, Buyback, Sell	$ 1.05	175%	$ 1,050.00
OMX	42.15	0	0	$ -	$ -			6/13/2007	Roll	$ -	-	$ -
OMX	38	0	0	$ -	$ -			7/17/2007	Close	$ -	-	$ -
PCLN	55.28 - 48	0	0	$ -	$ -			5/15/2007	Roll	$ -	-	$ -
PCLN	57.34 + 2.12	Oct	55	$ 4.30	$ 4.30			5/18/2007	Market letter	$ -	-	$ -
PCLN	62.67 + 1.57	Jul	55	$ 1.70	$ 0.75			5/23/2007	Sold, Buyback, Sell	$ 0.95	127%	$ 950.00
PCLN	60.34 + .06	Jun	55	$ 1.70	$ 0.05			6/12/2007	Sold, Buyback, Sell	$ 1.65	3300%	$ 1,650.00
PCLN	65.00 + 1.97	Jul	60	$ 2.10	$ 0.65			6/15/2007	Sold, Buyback, Sell	$ 1.45	223%	$ 1,450.00
PCLN	67.98 + 3.71	Jul	65	$ 2.30	$ 0.70			6/29/2007	Sold, Buyback, Sell	$ 1.60	229%	$ 1,600.00
PCLN	77.40 + 12.31	Aug	65	$ 2.30	$ 0.10			8/8/2007	Sold, Buyback, Sell	$ 2.20	2200%	$ 2,200.00
PCLN	80.11 + .94	Sep	70	$ 1.80	$ 0.70			8/23/2007	Sold, Buyback, Sell	$ 1.10	157%	$ 1,100.00
PCLN	84.19 + 2.76	Oct	75	$ 2.80	$ 1.55			9/12/2007	Sold, Buyback, Sell	$ 1.25	81%	$ 1,250.00
PCLN	94.96 + 2.14	Nov	80	$ 2.45	$ 1.50			10/10/2007	Sold, Buyback, Sell	$ 0.95	63%	$ 950.00
PCLN	98.09 + 13.82	Nov	85	$ 2.65	$ 0.30			11/9/2007	Sold, Buyback, Sell	$ 2.35	783%	$ 2,350.00
PCLN	103.89 + 19.56	Dec	85	$ 2.35	$ 1.75			11/9/2007	Sold, Buyback, Sell	$ 0.60	34%	$ 600.00
PCLN	115.00 + 1.99	Dec	90	$ 2.85	$ 0.60			11/29/2007	Sold, Buyback, Sell	$ 2.25	375%	$ 2,250.00

STOCK	TRADING INFORMATION	SHORT PUT		PURCHASE PRICE	PURCHASE SHORT SIDE CLOSED	SELL TO CLOSE FOR:	ORIGINAL PURCHASE PRICE	DATE CLOSED	Type of Notice	GAIN / (LOSS)	% RTN SHORT ONLY	$$$ BASED ON 10 CONTRACTS
PCLN	111.20 - 5.27	Jan	95	$ 2.45	$ 1.50			12/17/2007	Sold, Buyback, Sell	$ 0.95	63%	$ 950.00
PEIX	15.09 + 1.26	Sep	15	$ 1.75	$ 1.75			5/11/2007	Market letter	$ -		$ -
PEIX	13.89 - .11	0	0	$ -	$ -			7/17/2007	Roll	$ -		$ -
PETM	26.62 + 1.71	Apr	25	$ 1.80	$ 1.80			11/16/2007	Market letter			
PETM	26.90 + .89	Dec	25	$ 0.65	$ 0.35			11/28/2007	Sold, Buyback, Sell	$ 0.30	86%	$ 300.00
PLCM	31.80 + .48	Jun	35	$ 3.80	$ 3.25			6/11/2007	Sold, Buyback, Sell	$ 0.55	17%	$ 550.00
PLCM	35.51	Oct	35	$ 2.60	$ 2.60			7/13/2007	Market letter			
PLCM	35.02 + .54	0	0	$ -	$ -			7/17/2007	Roll	$ -		$ -
QCOM	0	Oct	43	$ 2.50	$ 2.50			5/11/2007	Market letter	$ -		$ -
QCOM	0	0	0	$ -	$ -			5/15/2007	Misc	$ -		$ -
QCOM	45.55 + 1.35	Jun	45	$ 2.10	$ 1.20			5/16/2007	Sold, Buyback, Sell	$ 0.90	75%	$ 900.00
QCOM	46.68 + .65	Jun	48	$ 2.70	$ 2.00			5/22/2007	Sold, Buyback, Sell	$ 0.70	35%	$ 700.00
QCOM	36.90 + .81	Jan	35	$ 3.20	$ 3.20			8/16/2007	Market letter			
QCOM	37.71 + .17	Sep	35	$ 1.55	$ 1.00			8/20/2007	Sold, Buyback, Sell	$ 0.55	55%	$ 550.00
QCOM	39.61 + .49	0	0	$ -	$ -			9/14/2007	Roll	$ -		$ -
QCOM	41.16 + .32	Oct	40	$ 1.65	$ 0.13			10/17/2007	Sold, Buyback, Sell	$ 1.52	1169%	$ 1,520.00
QCOM	42.57 + .79	Nov	40	$ 1.05	$ 0.48			10/31/2007	Sold, Buyback, Sell	$ 0.57	119%	$ 570.00
QCOM	38.72	0	0	$ -	$ -			12/19/2007	Roll	$ -		$ -
RTN	54	0	0	$ -	$ -			5/16/2007	Close	$ -		$ -
RTN	62.34 + 1.17	Jan	60	$ 2.35	$ 2.35			9/14/2007	Market letter			
RTN	62.55	Sep	63	$ 0.95	$ 0.70			9/19/2007	Sold, Buyback, Sell	$ 0.25	36%	$ 250.00
RTN	65.04 + 1.07	Feb	65	$ 3.25	$ 3.25			10/12/2007	Market letter			
RTN	61.59 + .07	0	0	$ -	$ -			11/12/2007	Roll	$ -		$ -
RTN	63.08 + 1.02	Dec	65	$ 4.75	$ 2.35			12/6/2007	Sold, Buyback, Sell	$ 2.40	102%	$ 2,400.00
RTN	64.50 + 1.53	Jan	65	$ 3.20	$ 2.20			12/12/2007	Sold, Buyback, Sell	$ 1.00	45%	$ 1,000.00
SEPR	53.77 + .46	0	0	$ -	$ -			5/15/2007	Roll	$ -		$ -
SEPR	47.1	0	0	$ -	$ -			6/13/2007	Roll	$ -		$ -
SGP	30.36 + .35	0	0	$ -	$ -			9/14/2007	Roll	$ -		$ -
SGP	32.21 - .94	Oct	30	$ 0.70	$ 0.05			10/17/2007	Sold, Buyback, Sell	$ 0.65	1300%	$ 650.00

STOCK	TRADING INFORMATION	SHORT PUT		PURCHASE PRICE	PURCHASE SHORT SIDE CLOSED	SELL TO CLOSE FOR:	ORIGINAL PURCHASE PRICE	DATE CLOSED	Type of Notice	GAIN / (LOSS)	% RTN SHORT ONLY	$$$$ BASED ON 10 CONTRACTS
SHRP	10.90 + 1.42	Nov	10	$ 1.30	1.30			5/25/2007	Market letter			
SHRP	13.39 + .89	Jun	10	$ 0.55	0.10			6/6/2007	Sold, Buyback, Sell	$ 0.45	450%	$ 450.00
SI	125. + 5.14 + .94	Jun	120	$ 2.55	1.45			5/18/2007	Sold, Buyback, Sell	$ 1.10	76%	$ 1,100.00
SI	131.24 + 1.58	Jul	125	$ 3.00	1.65			6/13/2007	Sold, Buyback, Sell	$ 1.35	82%	$ 1,350.00
SI	141.4 + 1.40	Jul	130	$ 2.75	0.50			6/26/2007	Sold, Buyback, Sell	$ 2.25	450%	$ 2,250.00
SI	119.6	0	0	-	-			9/18/2007	Roll	$ -		$ -
SI	132.84 + 1.09	Oct	125	$ 7.00	0.15			10/17/2007	Sold, Buyback, Sell	$ 6.85	4567%	$ 6,850.00
SII	54.00 + .94	Jun	55	$ 3.55	2.55			5/17/2007	Sold, Buyback, Sell	$ 1.00	39%	$ 1,000.00
SII	56.00 + 1.10	Jul	55	$ 3.15	2.15			5/23/2007	Sold, Buyback, Sell	$ 1.00	47%	$ 1,000.00
SII	57.00 + 1.00	Jul	60	$ 5.00	4.20			6/11/2007	Sold, Buyback, Sell	$ 0.80	19%	$ 800.00
SII	59.43 + 1.20	Jun	58	$ 1.15	0.05			6/14/2007	Sold, Buyback, Sell	$ 1.10	2200%	$ 1,100.00
SII	60.77 + 1.65	Jul	60	$ 2.40	1.90			6/28/2007	Sold, Buyback, Sell	$ 0.50	26%	$ 500.00
SII	62.00 + 1.15	Aug	60	$ 2.85	1.80			7/9/2007	Sold, Buyback, Sell	$ 1.05	58%	$ 1,050.00
SII	56.75 - 1.43	0	0	-	-			8/16/2007	Roll	$ -		$ -
SII	59.89 + 1.85	Sep	63	$ 7.50	4.75			8/17/2007	Sold, Buyback, Sell	$ 2.75	58%	$ 2,750.00
SII	69.59 + 1.34	Oct	65	$ 3.25	1.75			9/6/2007	Sold, Buyback, Sell	$ 1.50	86%	$ 1,500.00
SII	76.42 + 2.32	Oct	70	$ 3.65	0.20			10/15/2007	Sold, Buyback, Sell	$ 3.45	1725%	$ 3,450.00
SII	59.22 -.03	0	0	-	-			11/13/2007	Roll	$ -		$ -
SII	63.27 + 2.50	Dec	65	$ 7.50	4.20			11/20/2007	Sold, Buyback, Sell	$ 3.30	79%	$ 3,300.00
SII	66.00 + 1.47	Jan	65	$ 5.40	3.40			12/5/2007	Sold, Buyback, Sell	$ 2.00	59%	$ 2,000.00
SII	71.43	Apr	68	$ 4.60	4.60			12/21/2007	Market Letter			
SIRI	0	0	0	-	-			6/5/2007	Bonus	$ -		$ -
SIRI	2.86 + .11	Jun	3	-	-			6/15/2007	Misc	$ -		$ -
SIRI	3.22 + .10	Sep	3	$ 0.30	0.10			7/16/2007	Sold, Buyback, Sell	$ 0.20	200%	$ 200.00
SIRI	3.57 + .26	Sep	3	$ 0.13	0.05			9/12/2007	Sold, Buyback, Sell	$ 0.08	160%	$ 80.00
SIRI	3.63 + .16	Dec	4	$ 0.75	0.60			10/9/2007	Sold, Buyback, Sell	$ 0.15	25%	$ 150.00
SIRI	3.71 + .13	0	0	-	-			10/10/2007	Misc	$ -		$ -
SIRI	3.55 + .14	0	0	-	-			11/13/2007	Roll	$ -		$ -
SIRI	3.73 + .20	Dec	4	$ 0.65	0.55			11/30/2007	Sold, Buyback, Sell	$ 0.10	18%	$ 100.00
SLB	78.77	0	0	-	-			6/12/2007	Roll	$ -		$ -

STOCK	TRADING INFORMATION	SHORT PUT	PURCHASE PRICE	PURCHASE SHORT SIDE CLOSED	SELL TO CLOSE FOR:	ORIGINAL PURCHASE PRICE	DATE CLOSED	Type of Notice	GAIN / (LOSS)	% RTN SHORT ONLY	$$$$ BASED ON 10 CONTRACTS
SLB	90	Jul 75	$ 1.60	$ 0.05			7/18/2007	Sold, Buyback, Sell	$ 1.55	3100%	$ 1,550.00
SLB	92.42 + 1.38	Jan 85	$ 4.20	$ 4.20			8/24/2007	Market letter			
SLB	95.23 + 3.72	Sep 85	$ 0.90	$ 0.45			8/29/2007	Sold, Buyback, Sell	$ 0.45	100%	$ 450.00
SLB	112.33 + 2.49	Nov 95	$ 1.95	$ 0.65			10/15/2007	Sold, Buyback, Sell	$ 1.30	200%	$ 1,300.00
SLB	95.01 - 4.31	Jan 95			$ 6.85	$ 4.00	10/22/2007	Sell to close	$ 2.85	71%	$ 2,850.00
SLB	91.87 + .83	0 0	$ -	$ -			11/13/2007	Roll	$ -		$ -
SLB	93.87 + 2.35	Dec 100	$ 10.00	$ 7.40			11/20/2007	Sold, Buyback, Sell	$ 2.60	35%	$ 2,600.00
SLB	96.41 + 2.57	Jan 100	$ 8.65	$ 6.10			12/5/2007	Sold, Buyback, Sell	$ 2.55	42%	$ 2,550.00
SNE	55.35 + .81	May 55	$ 2.80	$ 1.10			5/9/2007	Sold, Buyback, Sell	$ 1.70	155%	$ 1,700.00
SNE	57.39 + 1.83	Jun 55	$ 1.55	$ 0.60			5/21/2007	Sold, Buyback, Sell	$ 0.95	158%	$ 950.00
SNE	59.57 + 2.18	Jul 55	$ 1.25	$ 0.75			5/22/2007	Sold, Buyback, Sell	$ 0.50	67%	$ 500.00
SNE	55.00 + 1.40	0 0	$ -	$ -			6/13/2007	Roll	$ -		$ -
SNE	51.5	0 0	$ -	$ -			7/18/2007	Close	$ -		$ -
SNE	50.00 + .55	Nov 50	$ 2.60	$ 1.40			11/1/2007	Sold, Buyback, Sell	$ 1.20	86%	$ 1,200.00
SNE	47.98 + 2.69	Jan 45	$ 1.40	$ 1.40			10/26/2007	Market letter			
SNE	51.07 + 1.99	Dec 50		$ 1.20			11/26/2007	Sold, Buyback, Sell	$ (1.20)	-100%	$ (1,200.00)
SNE	52.70 + 2.69	Jan 50		$ 1.35			11/27/2007	Sold, Buyback, Sell	$ (1.35)	-100%	$ (1,350.00)
SNE	55.87 + 1.18	Jan 55		$ 2.20			12/11/2007	Plat + note	$ (2.20)	-100%	$ (2,200.00)
SNE	55.68 + 1.04	Jan 60		$ 4.70			12/26/2007	Sold, Buyback, Sell	$ (4.70)	-100%	$ (4,700.00)
SNY	48.09 + 1.14	Mar 48	$ 2.65	$ 1.30			6/4/2007	Sold, Buyback, Sell	$ 1.35	104%	$ 1,350.00
SNY	42.68	0 0	$ -	$ -			7/18/2007	Roll	$ -		$ -
SUN	80.73 + 1.11	Jun 80	$ 4.50	$ 1.00			6/11/2007	Sold, Buyback, Sell	$ 3.50	350%	$ 3,500.00
TAP	91.5	0 0	$ -	$ -			7/18/2007	Close	$ -		$ -
TAP	88.68	Jan 85	$ 3.20	$ 3.20			9/7/2007	Market letter			
TAP	95.89 + 2.01	Oct 90	$ 2.70	$ 0.85			9/17/2007	Sold, Buyback, Sell	$ 1.85	218%	$ 1,850.00
TAP	57.00 + 6.13 2:1 split	Nov 50	$ 1.40	$ 0.30			10/9/2007	Sold, Buyback, Sell	$ 1.10	367%	$ 1,100.00
TAP	57.24 + 1.07	Nov 55	$ 1.25	$ 0.85			10/26/2007	Sold, Buyback, Sell	$ 0.40	47%	$ 400.00
TAP	51.16 - .89	0 0	$ -	$ -			12/17/2007	Roll	$ -		$ -
TASR	15.00 + .34	Sep 15	$ 1.20	$ 0.60			9/6/2007	Sold, Buyback, Sell	$ 0.60	100%	$ 600.00
TASR	18.92 + .36	Nov 18	$ 1.70	$ 1.05			10/9/2007	Sold, Buyback, Sell	$ 0.65	62%	$ 650.00
TASR	16.46 - .32	0 0	$ -	$ -			10/26/2007	Roll	$ -		$ -

STOCK	TRADING INFORMATION	SHORT PUT		PURCHASE PRICE	PURCHASE SHORT SIDE CLOSED	SELL TO CLOSE FOR:	ORIGINAL PURCHASE PRICE	DATE CLOSED	Type of Notice	GAIN / (LOSS)	% RTN SHORT ONLY	$$$ BASED ON 10 CONTRACTS
TASR	0	0	0	$ -	$ -			12/19/2007	Close	$ -	-	$ -
TDS	69.79 + 1.33	Oct	70	$ 2.85	$ 1.50			10/12/2007	Sold, Buyback, Sell	$ 1.35	90%	$ 1,350.00
TGT	60.16 + 1.56	Oct	60	$ 3.20	$ 3.20			5/25/2007	Market letter			
TGT	62.43 + 1.35	Jun	63	$ 2.60	$ 0.85			5/31/2007	Sold, Buyback, Sell	$ 1.75	206%	$ 1,750.00
TGT	63.82 + .51	Jul	63	$ 1.70	$ 1.15			6/20/2007	Sold, Buyback, Sell	$ 0.55	48%	$ 550.00
TGT	66.48 + 2.47	Aug	63	$ 1.75	$ 1.15			7/6/2007	Sold, Buyback, Sell	$ 0.60	52%	$ 600.00
TGT	70.10 + 4.5	Aug	65	$ 1.95	$ 0.95			7/12/2007	Sold, Buyback, Sell	$ 1.00	105%	$ 1,000.00
TGT	57.97 + .01	0	0	$ -	$ -			8/16/2007	Roll	$ -	-	$ -
TGT	62.30 + 2.2	Sep	68	$ 11.00	$ 5.60			8/22/2007	Sold, Buyback, Sell	$ 5.40	96%	$ 5,400.00
TGT	66.28 + 1.19	Nov	65	$ 3.70	$ 2.45			10/5/2007	Sold, Buyback, Sell	$ 1.25	51%	$ 1,250.00
TGT	54.21 + 2.41	Apr	53	$ 5.30	$ 5.30			11/23/2007	Market letter			
TGT	56.70 + 1.48	Dec	53	$ 2.30	$ 1.85			11/27/2007	Sold, Buyback, Sell	$ 0.45	24%	$ 450.00
TGT	58.79 + 1.79	Jan	53	$ 2.80	$ 1.75			11/28/2007	Sold, Buyback, Sell	$ 1.05	60%	$ 1,050.00
TM	111.27 + 1.54	Nov	100	$ 0.70	$ 0.20			10/29/2007	Sold, Buyback, Sell	$ 0.50	250%	$ 500.00
TM	108.98 + 1.95	00Jan	100	$ 1.75	$ 1.75			10/19/2007	Market letter			
TM	116.00 + 4.00	Dec	105	$ 1.50	$ 0.95			11/7/2007	Sold, Buyback, Sell	$ 0.55	58%	$ 550.00
TM	106.5	0	0	$ -	$ -			12/19/2007	Roll	$ -	-	$ -
TXU	66.21 - .30	May	65	$ 0.80	$ 0.05			5/14/2007	Sold, Buyback, Sell	$ 0.75	1500%	$ 750.00
TXU	67.41 - .13	Jun	65	$ 0.50	$ 0.05	.		6/12/2007	Sold, Buyback, Sell	$ 0.45	900%	$ 450.00
TXU	67.34	Jul	65	$ 0.30	$ 0.05			7/18/2007	Sold, Buyback, Sell	$ 0.25	500%	$ 250.00
UNP	118.08 + .67	May	120	$ 3.90	$ 2.35			5/15/2007	Sold, Buyback, Sell	$ 1.55	66%	$ 1,550.00
UNP	119.04 + 2.13	Jun	120	$ 4.40	$ 3.20			5/25/2007	Sold, Buyback, Sell	$ 1.20	38%	$ 1,200.00
UNP	119.47 + 1.65	Jul	120	$ 4.60	$ 2.80			7/12/2007	Sold, Buyback, Sell	$ 1.80	64%	$ 1,800.00
UNP	122.89 + 2.09	Jul	120	$ 4.60	$ 0.90			7/16/2007	Sold, Buyback, Sell	$ 3.70	411%	$ 3,700.00
UNP	128.36 + 4.31	Aug	120	$ 2.65	$ 1.40			7/18/2007	Sold, Buyback, Sell	$ 1.25	89%	$ 1,250.00
UNP	101.57 - 6.03	0	0	$ -	$ -			8/16/2007	Close	$ -	-	$ -
UNP	110.84 + 4.91	0	0	$ -	$ -			8/20/2007	Bonus	$ -	-	$ -
UNP	112.52 + 2.9	Oct	105	$ 2.65	$ 1.65			8/22/2007	Sold, Buyback, Sell	$ 1.00	61%	$ 1,000.00
UNP	112.24 + 3.55	Oct	105	$ 3.00	$ 1.95			9/13/2007	Sold, Buyback, Sell	$ 1.05	54%	$ 1,050.00
UNP	119.00 + 2.82	Nov	110	$ 3.05	$ 1.35			10/17/2007	Sold, Buyback, Sell	$ 1.70	126%	$ 1,700.00
UNP	124.97 + 2.35	Nov	115	$ 2.60	$ 1.10			10/22/2007	Sold, Buyback, Sell	$ 1.50	136%	$ 1,500.00

STOCK	TRADING INFORMATION	SHORT PUT	PURCHASE PRICE	PURCHASE SHORT SIDE CLOSED	SELL TO CLOSE FOR:	ORIGINAL PURCHASE PRICE	DATE CLOSED	Type of Notice	GAIN / (LOSS)	% RTN SHORT ONLY	$$$ BASED ON 10 CONTRACTS
UNP	128.04	Dec 115	$ 2.55	$ 1.65			11/1/2007	Sold, Buyback, Sell	$ 0.90	55%	$ 900.00
UNP	129.00 + 2.26	Dec 120	$ 2.70	$ 0.60			12/5/2007	Sold, Buyback, Sell	$ 2.10	350%	$ 2,100.00
UNP	135.71 + 1.76	Jan 120	$ 2.00	$ 0.85			12/7/2007	Sold, Buyback, Sell	$ 1.15	135%	$ 1,150.00
WAG	44.17	0 0	$ -	$ -			6/11/2007	Roll	$ -		$ -
VRSN	31.72 + 1.27	Dec 30	$ 1.75	$ 1.75			6/29/2007	Market letter			
VRSN	32.38 + .85	Jul 33	$ 1.35	$ 1.00			7/2/2007	Sold, Buyback, Sell	$ 0.35	35%	$ 350.00
VRSN	34.00 + 1.05	Aug 33	$ 1.45	$ 0.95			7/13/2007	Sold, Buyback, Sell	$ 0.50	53%	$ 500.00
VRSN	30.05	Aug 30	$ -	$ -			8/15/2007	Misc	$ -		$ -
VRSN	34.18 + .78	Oct 33	$ 1.05	$ 0.15			10/16/2007	Sold, Buyback, Sell	$ 0.90	600%	$ 900.00
VRSN	32.9	0 0	$ -	$ -			11/13/2007	Roll	$ -		$ -
VRSN	35.17 + 1.90	Dec 35	$ 2.70	$ 1.35			11/16/2007	Sold, Buyback, Sell	$ 1.35	100%	$ 1,350.00
VRSN	37.25 + 1.20	Jan 35	$ 1.95	$ 1.35			11/19/2007	Sold, Buyback, Sell	$ 0.60	44%	$ 600.00
VRSN	0	0 0	$ -	$ -			11/26/2004	Roll	$ -		$ -
VRSN	38.00 + 1.25	Dec 38	$ 1.85	$ 1.25			11/26/2007	Sold, Buyback, Sell	$ 0.60	48%	$ 600.00
WFMI	40.04 - 5.77	Aug 50			$ 9.40	.25 cr	5/10/2007	Sell to close			
WFMI	38.74 + .5	0 0	$ -	$ -			6/13/2007	Roll	$ -		$ -
WFMI	40.75 + .78	Jul 40	$ 2.30	$ 0.40			7/18/2007	Sold, Buyback, Sell	$ 1.90	475%	$ 1,900.00
WY	81.43 + 1.20	0 0	$ -	$ -			6/13/2007	Roll	$ -		$ -
WY	0	0 0	$ -	$ -			7/19/2007	Misc	$ -		$ -
WY	73.42 + 1.42	Jan 80			$ 10.20	5.10	7/30/2007	Sell to close	$ 5.10	100%	$ 5,100.00
WY	70.80 + 1.83	0 0	$ -	$ -			9/18/2007	Roll	$ -		$ -
WY	75.90 + 3.10	Apr 70	$ 3.90	$ 3.90			12/7/2007	Market letter			
YHOO	26.07 - 1.45	0 0	$ -	$ -			7/18/2007	Close	$ -		$ -

*　　*　　*　　*　　*　　*　　*　　*　　*

Appendix 5: 2008 Year Track Record

Performance for the Year 2008:　Short Put Sells as of February, 2008 follows:

STOCK	TRADING INFORMATION	SHORT PUT	PURCHASE PRICE		PURCHASE SHORT SIDE CLOSED		SELL TO CLOSE FOR:	ORIGINAL PURCHASE PRICE	DATE CLOSED	Type of Notice	GAIN / LOSS		% RTN SHORT ONLY	$$$$ BASED ON 10 CONTRACTS	
AAPL	12.05 - 4.31	0	0	$ -	$ -				2/6/2008	Roll, change position					
ABT	59.27	Jan	58	$ 1.00	$ 0.45				1/8/2008	Sold, Buyback	$	0.55	122%	$	550.00
ABT	60.76 + .96	Feb	58	$ 1.10	$ 0.80				1/11/2008	Sold, Buyback	$	0.30	38%	$	300.00
ACL	0	0	0	$ -	$ -				1/2/2008	Note from Think or Swim					
ACL	142.26 + 2.01	0	0	$ -	$ -				1/9/2008	Close					
ACL	150.00 + 9.83	Mar	130	$ 1.30	$ 0.80				2/7/2008	Sold, Buyback	$	0.50	63%	$	500.00
ACL	148.74 - 5.71	0	0	$ -	$ -				2/8/2008	Buying opportunity					
ADBE	34.07	0	0	$ -	$ -				1/22/2008	Miscellaneous					
ADBE	35	0	0	$ -	$ -				1/22/2008	Roll					
AGN	68.00 + 1.87	Jan	68	$ 2.30	$ 1.30				1/10/2008	Sold, Buyback	$	1.00	77%	$	1,000.00
AGN	66.75 + 3.63	0	0	$ -	$ -				1/31/2008	Roll					
APA	110.00 + 2.50	Jan	100	$ 1.00	$ 0.70				1/2/2008	Sold, Buyback	$	0.30	43%	$	300.00
APA	90.49 - 5.35	Apr	90	$ -	$ -		$ 3.80	$ 5.00	1/22/2008	Bought, stc, b	$	(1.20)	-24%	$	(1,200.00)
APA	100.13 + 2.36	0	0	$ -	$ -				2/8/2008	Roll					
APA	110.00 + 3.90	Mar	100	$ 4.20	$ 1.35				2/19/2008	Sold, Buyback	$	2.85	211%	$	2,850.00
AVY	48.57 - 1.06	0	0	$ -	$ -				1/11/2008	Roll					
AVY	50.51 + 3.03	Feb	50	$ 2.25	$ 1.10				1/29/2008	Sold, Buyback	$	1.15	105%	$	1,150.00
AVY	52.58 + .83	Mar	50	$ 2.05	$ 1.35				2/1/2008	Sold, Buyback	$	0.70	52%	$	700.00
AZN	45.37 + .40	0	0	$ -	$ -				1/11/2008	Roll					
AZN	38.64 - 2.21	Apr	45				$ 2.85	$ 3.20	2/7/2008	Bought, stc, b	$	(0.35)	-11%	$	(350.00)
BA	81.73 - 1.14	Jan	95				$ 0.85	$ 9.00	1/8/2008	Bought, stc, b	$	(8.15)	-91%	$	(8,150.00)
BA	84.50 + 3.87	0	0	$ -	$ -				2/12/2008	Close					
BBY	47.00 - .37	0	0	$ -	$ -				2/12/2008	Roll					
BWA	43.02 + .10	0	0	$ -	$ -				1/15/2008	Roll					
BWA	42.2	0	0	$ -	$ -				1/16/2008	Miscellaneous					
BWA	0	0	0	$ -	$ -				1/17/2008	Miscellaneous					
BWA	46.40 + 1.65	Feb	45	$ 2.85	$ 2.10				1/22/2008	Sold, Buyback	$	0.75	36%	$	750.00
CL	76.90 + 3.40	Feb	75	$ 0.85	$ 0.40				1/31/2008	Sold, Buyback	$	0.45	113%	$	450.00
COP	75.97 + .58	0	0	$ -	$ -				2/11/2008	Roll					
COP	80.82 + 1.77	Mar	85	$ 11.10	$ 5.35				2/19/2008	Sold, Buyback	$	5.75	107%	$	5,750.00
COST	65.34 - .89	0	0	$ -	$ -				1/31/2008	Roll					
DLX	28.5	Jan	35				$ 1.45	$ 3.70	1/7/2008	Bought, stc, b	$	(2.25)	-61%	$	(2,250.00)

STOCK	TRADING INFORMATION	SHORT PUT	PURCHASE PRICE	PURCHASE SHORT SIDE CLOSED	SELL TO CLOSE FOR:	ORIGINAL PURCHASE PRICE	DATE CLOSED	Type of Notice	GAIN / LOSS	% RTN SHORT ONLY	$$$$ BASED ON 10 CONTRACTS
DO	115.00 + 4.50	Mar	100	$ 0.85			2/19/2008	Sold, Buyback	$ 0.85	100%	$ 850.00
DVN	90.00 + 1.10	Jan	90	$ 2.45			1/2/2008	Sold, Buyback	$ 1.65	67%	$ 1,650.00
DVN	93.36 + 1.50	Feb	90	$ 2.70			1/3/2008	Sold, Buyback	$ 1.35	50%	$ 1,350.00
DVN	83.31 + 2.24	Apr	80	$ -	$ 2.20	$ 2.35	1/28/2008	Bought, stc, b	$ (0.15)	-6%	$ (150.00)
DVN	90.00 + 2.09	0	0	$ -			2/8/2008	Roll			
DVN	96.00 + 2.87	Mar	95	$ 3.50			2/19/2008	Sold, Buyback	$ 3.30	94%	$ 3,300.00
ESLR	0	0	0	$ -			1/2/2008	Note from Think or Swim			
ESLR	13.6	0	0	$ -			1/16/2008	Miscellaneous			
ESLR	10.64 + .53	0	0	$ -			2/13/2008	Roll			
ESRX	74.65 + 1.60	Jan	70	$ 0.50			1/3/2008	Sold, Buyback	$ 2.25	450%	$ 2,250.00
ESRX	75.00 + 1.40	Jan	70	$ 0.40			1/7/2008	Sold, Buyback	$ 2.35	588%	$ 2,350.00
GD	86.63 - 2.20	0	0	$ -			1/11/2008	Roll			
GD	88.57 + .01	0	0	$ -			1/14/2008	Roll			
GOOG	506.79	0	0	$ -			2/6/2008	Bonus trade/Cancelled			
GOOG	502.33 - 4.46	0	0	$ -			2/6/2008	Correction/Cancel			
GOOG	524.65 + 6.98	Mar	450	$ 3.00			2/13/2008	Sold, Buyback	$ 6.00	200%	$ 6,000.00
GPRO	62.14 - 1.26	0	0	$ -			1/11/2008	Close			
GRMN	89.35 + 1.83	Jan	95	$ -	$ 2.90	$ 6.55	1/7/2008	Bought, stc, b	$ (3.65)	-56%	$ (3,650.00)
GRMN	87.24 - 1.15	0	0	$ -			1/7/2008	Roll			
GRMN	60.35 - 5.27	0	0	$ -			1/16/2008	Close			
GRMN	0	0	0	$ -			1/16/2008	Close			
GRMN	65.08 - 4.63	Feb	90	$ -	$ 6.55	$ 21.00	2/5/2008	Bought, stc, b	$ (14.45)	-69%	$ (14,450.00)
GT	24.51	0	0	$ -			1/11/2008	Roll			
GT	25.78 + .71	Feb	25	$ 1.10			1/28/2008	Sold, Buyback	$ 0.55	50%	$ 550.00
GT	27.00 + 1.68	Mar	25	$ 0.75			2/14/2008	Sold, Buyback	$ 1.00	133%	$ 1,000.00
GT	27.45 + .50	Mar	25	$ 0.70			2/19/2008	Sold, Buyback	$ 1.05	150%	$ 1,050.00
HAL	38.40 + .49	Jan	38	$ 0.55			1/2/2008	Sold, Buyback	$ 0.50	91%	$ 500.00
HOG	39.74 - .75	0	0	$ -			1/15/2008	Roll, later cancelled			
HOG	39.97 + 1.25	0	0	$ -			1/16/2008	Roll			
HOG	41.05 + 2.50	Feb	43	$ 2.25			1/31/2008	Sold, Buyback	$ 1.25	56%	$ 1,250.00
HOG	40.64 + 2.13	0	0	$ -			2/1/2008	Close			
IBM	105.00 + 8.30	0	0	$ -			1/14/2008	Roll			

STOCK	TRADING INFORMATION	SHORT PUT	PURCHASE PRICE	PURCHASE SHORT SIDE CLOSED	SELL TO CLOSE FOR:	ORIGINAL PURCHASE PRICE	DATE CLOSED	Type of Notice	GAIN / LOSS	% RTN SHORT ONLY	$$$$ BASED ON 10 CONTRACTS
IBM	105.64 + 4.74	0	0 $ -	$ -			1/18/2008	Miscellaneous			
IBM	106.86 + 1.72	0	0 $ -	$ -			2/12/2008	Roll			
IMCL	43.83 + 1.22	Feb	40 $ 1.05	$ 0.70			1/29/2008	Sold, Buyback	$ 0.35	50%	$ 350.00
IVGN	94.38 + 1.85	Feb	90 $ 3.35	$ 2.40			1/8/2008	Sold, Buyback	$ 0.95	40%	$ 950.00
IVGN	96.75 + 2.31	Feb	95 $ 4.50	$ 3.50			1/17/2008	Sold, Buyback	$ 1.00	29%	$ 1,000.00
IVGN	87.77 + .25	Feb	90 $	$	$ 1.20	$ 3.75	1/30/2008	Bought, stc, b	$ (2.55)	-68%	$ (2,550.00)
IVGN	88.82 + 5.39	0	0 $ -	$ -			2/6/2008	Roll			
IVGN	0	0	0 $ -	$ -			2/6/2008	Roll			
LMT	108.00 + 1.55	Feb	100 $ 0.90	$ 0.35			1/30/2008	Sold, Buyback	$ 0.55	157%	$ 550.00
LMT	109.05 + .93	Feb	100 $ 0.90	$ 0.20			2/4/2008	Sold, Buyback	$ 0.70	350%	$ 700.00
LMT	107.5	0	0 $ -	$ -			2/12/2008	Roll			
MRO	55.00 + .52	0	0 $ -	$ -			1/14/2008	Roll			
MRO	52.56 + 1.71	Mar	45 $ 0.65	$ 0.35			2/19/2008	Sold, Buyback	$ 0.30	86%	$ 300.00
NKE	61.54 - .20	0	0 $ -	$ -			1/7/2008	Roll			
NKE	57.06	0	0 $ -	$ -			1/16/2008	Sell			
NOC	80.45 + .58	0	0 $ -	$ -			1/14/2008	Roll			
NOC	80.00 + .49	Feb	80 $ 2.40	$ 0.95			2/12/2008	Sold, Buyback	$ 1.45	153%	$ 1,450.00
NOK	0	0	0 $ -	$ -			2/12/2008	Roll			
NOK	36.80 + .67	Mar	35 $ 1.75	$ 1.20			2/12/2008	Sold, Buyback	$ 0.55	46%	$ 550.00
OI	49.55 + 6.20	Feb	45 $ 1.41	$ 0.50			1/31/2008	Sold, Buyback	$ 0.91	182%	$ 910.00
OI	53.00 + 2.40	Mar	50 $ 2.95	$ 1.90			2/1/2008	Sold, Buyback	$ 1.05	55%	$ 1,050.00
OI	0	0	0 $ -	$ -			2/14/2008	Roll			
OI	56.00 + 1.69	Mar	55 $ 4.20	$ 2.40			2/14/2008	Sold, Buyback	$ 1.80	75%	$ 1,800.00
PCLN	99.83 + 3.58	0	0 $ -	$ -			1/14/2008	Roll			
PCLN	105.64 - 1.26	Feb	100 $ 7.60	$ 4.50			2/4/2008	Sold, Buyback	$ 3.10	69%	$ 3,100.00
PCLN	103.35 + .35	0	0 $ -	$ -			2/13/2008	Miscellaneous			
PCLN	113.52 + 11.27	0	0 $ -	$ -			2/15/2008	Close			
PETM	20.50 - .79	0	0 $ -	$ -			1/15/2008	Roll			
PETM	22.11 + .53	Apr	25 $	$	$ 1.80	$ 2.00	1/22/2008	Bought, stc, b	$ (0.20)	-10%	$ (200.00)
PETM	23.58 + .71	Feb	23 $ 2.25	$ 0.55			2/1/2008	Sold, Buyback	$ 1.70	309%	$ 1,700.00
RIG (GSF)	139.21 - 3.25	0	0 $ -	$ -			1/7/2008	Close			
RTN	61.62 + .83	0	0 $ -	$ -			1/14/2008	Roll			

STOCK	TRADING INFORMATION	SHORT PUT	PURCHASE PRICE	PURCHASE SHORT SIDE CLOSED	SELL TO CLOSE FOR:	ORIGINAL PURCHASE PRICE	DATE CLOSED	Type of Notice	GAIN / LOSS	% RTN SHORT ONLY	$$$$ BASED ON 10 CONTRACTS
RTN	66.84 + 1.27	Feb	$ 63	$ 1.86	$ 0.05			2/11/2008	Sold, Buyback	$ 1.81	3620%	$ 1,810.00
SII	68.96 + .94	0	$ 0	$ -				1/14/2008	Roll			
SII	54.77 - 2.14	Apr	$ 68		$ 4.60	$ 10.90	1/30/2008	Bought, stc, b	$ (6.30)	-58%	$ (6,300.00)
SII	55.01 - 1.85	0	$ 0	$ -				1/30/2008	Roll			
SIRI	2.90 - .03	0	$ 0	$ -				1/14/2008	Close			
SLB	99.70 + 1.53	Jan	$ 105	$ 9.60	$ 6.60			1/2/2008	Sold, Buyback	$ 3.00	45%	$ 3,000.00
SLB	82.96 + 1.46	0	$ 0	$ -				2/13/2008	Close			
SLB	82.96 + 1.46	0	$ 0	$ -				2/13/2008	Correction			
SNE	56.80 + 2.64	Feb	$ 55	$ 2.40	$ 1.90			1/9/2008	Sold, Buyback	$ 0.50	26%	$ 500.00
TAP	51.69 + 1.00	0	$ 0	$ -				1/7/2008	Roll			
TAP	51.90 + 1.21	Jan	$ 55	$ 5.00	$ 3.30			1/7/2008	Sold, Buyback	$ 1.70	52%	$ 1,700.00
TAP	49.28 - .42	0	$ 0	$ -				1/14/2008	Close			
TGT	49.75 - .22	0	$ 0	$ -				1/14/2008	Roll			
TGT	52.96 + 2.88	Feb	$ 55	$ 6.00	$ 3.75			1/22/2008	Sold, Buyback	$ 2.25	60%	$ 2,250.00
TGT	57.05 + 1.65	Mar	$ 55	$ 5.05	$ 2.90			2/4/2008	Sold, Buyback	$ 2.15	74%	$ 2,150.00
TM	104.34 + 1.41	0	$ 0	$ -				1/14/2008	Close			
TM	108.00 + 3.27	Feb	$ 95	$ 1.10	$ 0.35			1/31/2008	Sold, Buyback	$ 0.75	214%	$ 750.00
TM	109.80 + 1.48	Mar	$ 100	$ 1.80	$ 0.90			2/4/2008	Sold, Buyback	$ 0.90	100%	$ 900.00
TM	111.00 + 1.48	Mar	$ 100	$ 1.80	$ 1.15			2/15/2008	Sold, Buyback	$ 0.65	57%	$ 650.00
TM	117.00 + 6.00	Mar	$ 110	$ 2.10	$ 1.45			2/19/2008	Sold, Buyback	$ 0.65	45%	$ 650.00
UNP	114.26 + 1.97	0	$ 0	$ -				1/16/2008	Roll			
UNP	124.31 + 3.35	0	$ 0	$ -				1/31/2008	Roll			
VRSN	32.92 + .51	Mar	$ 33		$ 0.60	$ 0.95	1/28/2008	Bought, stc, b	$ (0.35)	-37%	$ (350.00)
VRSN	35.65 + .33	Feb	$ 35	$ 1.40	$ 0.25			2/12/2008	Sold, Buyback	$ 1.15	460%	$ 1,150.00
WMT	51.00 + 1.84	Feb	$ 50	$ 1.40	$ 0.70			1/31/2008	Sold, Buyback	$ 0.70	100%	$ 700.00
WMT	51.04 + .30	0	$ 0	$ -				2/1/2008	Miscellaneous			
WMT	50.20 + .60	Feb	$ 50	$ 1.40	$ 0.60			2/12/2008	Sold, Buyback	$ 0.80	133%	$ 800.00
WY	68.71 + .71	0	$ 0	$ -				1/14/2008	Roll			
WY	64.00 + .20	0	$ 0	$ -				2/12/2008	Roll			
YHOO	23.75 + .39	0	$ 0	$ -				1/14/2008	Roll			
YHOO	28.85 + 9.97	Feb	$ 25	$ 2.63	$ 0.45			2/1/2008	Sold, Buyback	$ 2.18	484%	$ 2,180.00

Index

Acknowledgements   12, 15

Advisory service   4-6, 10, 11, 13, 19, 66, 79, 80, 84, 87, 102, 128, 132

Ask   50, 117-122, 126

Ascent Option Spreads   3, 4, 13, 15, 19, 20, 131, 185

Assignment   4, 113, 129, 150, 151

At the market   3, 117, 120

At-The-Money (ATM)   56, 57, 153

Bear Spread   151

Bull Spread   151, 152, 155

Bid   50, 117-122, 126

Calendar Spread   10, 131, 143, 145, 147-149, 152

Call   21, 24, 29, 37, 62, 67, 70, 94, 95, 101, 119, 128, 129, 132, 135, 136, 146, 147, 150-158

Call buyer   37, 39, 40, 43-45, 51-53, 59, 60, 66, 70, 77

Call options   12, 39-41, 44, 45, 51-56, 59, 60, 65, 67, 68, 88, 89, 141, 142, 151

Call seller   37, 40, 43, 44, 60, 66, 67, 70

Call spread   94, 96, 155

Chicago Board of Options Exchange (CBOE)   50, 83, 85, 117, 119, 126, 136

Contract   4, 12, 29, 37, 43, 45, 49, 50, 52, 55, 56, 65, 67, 70, 75, 76, 79, 83, 84, 92, 96, 97, 101, 103, 107, 109, 110, 112, 116, 119, 126, 127, 135, 136, 144-146, 148, 153

Conversion Table   123

Copyright   10, 12

Covered Calls   93, 129, 150-154

Covered Spreads   9, 29, 93, 152

Credit   3, 4, 25, 76, 79-81, 85-89, 94, 96-98, 119, 128, 142, 145, 146, 148-150

Debit   3, 4, 25, 76, 79, 83-88, 96-98, 103, 106, 107, 116, 119, 126-128, 135, 144, 147, 150

Diagonal Put   3, 10

Disclaimer   10-12

Ellsworth, Paul G.   9, 10, 13, 15, 20, 133, 187

Equis.com   19, 20, 185

Exercise of Option   39, 44, 45, 52, 53, 56, 57, 61, 65, 68-70, 76-78, 80, 81, 83, 86, 91, 102-105, 107, 113, 144, 151

Foreword   12, 19-20

Free cash   91

Good 'Til Cancelled (GTC)   117

Graphs   13, 19, 63, 155-158

Hecht, Mervyn L.   3, 21

Intrinsic Value   55-58, 77, 81, 92, 141, 145, 149

In-The-Money (ITM)   53-58, 62, 68, 77, 80, 81, 86-89, 105, 128, 129, 145, 150, 152, 153

Investor   19, 21, 23, 31, 60, 71, 98, 100, 136, 143, 145, 152, 154

Margin   13, 78, 80, 88, 91-98, 102-104, 106-108, 111, 128, 135-138, 146-148

Naked   29, 60, 61, 93

Objective   47, 62

Option Clearing Corporation (OCC)   5, 29, 128

Index

Option Exercised   39, 44, 45, 52, 53, 56, 57, 61, 65, 68-70, 76-78, 80-83, 86, 91, 102-105, 107, 113, 144, 151

Option Profitability Trade Log   13, 91, 101-116, 127

Option Strategies   3, 10, 13, 19, 21, 31, 82, 135

Option Trading   5, 10, 12, 13, 20, 21, 23, 27, 29, 31, 35, 47, 59, 65, 66, 69, 70, 75, 77, 83, 84, 91, 96, 98, 101, 119, 121, 125, 128, 131, 132, 141, 142, 150

Options Price Chart   119

Other-People's-Money (OPM)   67, 116, 131, 148, 149

Out-of-The-Money (OTM)   3, 24, 55-58, 62, 68, 76, 77, 81, 83-85, 131, 146

Ownership   55, 70

Preface   12, 21

Profitability Trade Log   13, 91, 101-116, 123, 127

Pro-Option-Profits.com   5

Purchase   12, 43-45, 51

Put   21, 23-25, 29, 37, 57, 61, 62, 75-87, 92-96, 101-114, 119, 126, 127, 129, 132, 135-141, 143-146, 148-151, 153-156

Put buyer   25, 37, 41-44, 47, 61, 65, 153

Put options 12, 41, 47, 55, 57, 61, 65-67, 75-77, 80-87, 106, 113, 114, 138, 140,141, 151

Put option spread   3, 4, 62, 75, 76, 79, 80, 94, 96, 107, 152, 126, 131, 144, 149, 153

Put seller   37, 41, 43, 61, 62, 66, 67, 78, 81, 153

Regulation T   19, 93-95

Reuters Financial News Service   19, 163

Risk   9, 11, 12, 21, 24, 31- 35, 51, 53, 59 - 62, 67-71, 76-78, 80-83, 85, 86, 88, 91-93, 96-98, 105, 107, 116, 122, 131, 140, 143, 144, 148, 151

Risk Management   12, 35, 65, 69-71, 84, 85, 91, 107, 116, 122, 140, 154

Security Exchange Commission (SEC)   2, 27, 31

Selling short   4, 12, 67, 69, 77

Shapray, Don   3, 4, 6, 9, 10, 13, 15, 19, 132, 185

Spread   9, 19, 21, 23, 25, 29, 62, 76-81, 83-88, 93, 94, 96-98, 102, 103, 107, 111, 116, 119-122, 125-128, 135, 140, 144, 149

Spread Option Trades   13, 23, 76, 83, 84, 93, 96, 97

Static   24, 47, 99

Strategy   3-5, 10-13, 15, 19-21, 24, 27, 29, 31, 35, 45, 47, 55, 61, 65, 67, 82, 85-88, 99, 117, 120, 121, 128, 131, 132, 133, 135, 136, 142, 143, 145, 146, 148, 149, 154

Testimonials   3-6, 12

Thinkorswim.com (TOS)   4,

Time Value   3, 4, 55, 58, 81, 141, 142, 151

Thomson Reuters   19, 185

Track Record   13, 20, 66, 91, 101, 121, 133, 159, 178

Trader   5, 27, 31, 49, 66, 78, 79, 98, 99

Trading fees   4-6, 51, 59, 68, 77, 91, 92, 94, 95, 102, 103, 105, 107, 111, 113, 114, 136

Volatile   33, 47, 58, 59, 65, 88, 99, 129, 131, 135, 136, 138, 140

Warning   10-12

www.800option.com   20, 101, 132, 163

About Don Shapray, Author

Don Shapray, CEO of **Ascent Option Spreads** has an interesting background.

Mr. Shapray is also, the stock picking and Options strategic chief guru of **Shapray Option Trading**, one of the world's most innovative stock market research and analysis publishing firms. A former Nation Options Manager with Charles Schwab who hosted a Hollywood, California based stock market television show on the stock market channel. His unique perspective on public company analysis is a global publishing sensation, having reached investors in places as diverse as Hong Kong, Australia, Germany, Singapore, Taiwan, India, and Canada. His landmark yacht racing to public company analysis performance, was in the top 5% of all stock market newsletter services, in terms of track record.

Ascent Option Spreads is an integrated stock picking and options strategic services firm focusing solely on investing leadership (professional as well as personal). It offers a complete line of elite speaking services, newsletter program and learning tools to help investors maximize productivity, attain profitability, and attain true market success. **Recently, Thomson Reuters (a division of the highly respected Reuters Financial News Service) sought out Don Shapray to be a *Partner* and an *Option Spread Educator* for their worldwide established paying clientele. (For further information visit: www.equis.com and select: "partners".)**

Also, new wave portfolio managers and ex-brokerage executives are embracing Donald's unique stock market success philosophy. To schedule a print, radio or television interview with Mr. Shapray, please contact us at **1-866-6-SPREAD (777323).**

About Paul G. Ellsworth, Author

Paul G. Ellsworth, author of **Tai Chi Chuan Silk Reeling Exercises** and **Tai Chi Silk Reeling Exercises** (DVD) is a consultant and Tai Chi-Qigong teacher. He has a BA degree in Religion with minors in Biological & Chemical Sciences from Florida State University.

He has taken graduate courses in Business Law, Capitalism & Human Values, Intergovernmental Relations, Science, Technology, & Society.

He was a Florida state licensed life insurance, health insurance, & variable annuities agent & NASD series 6 mutual funds agent for a **Fortune 100** financial institution; the Florida agency **#1** for 4 (or more) years.

He is currently a Florida state licensed real estate agent. He was consistently in the **top 25%** of the sales force for a **Fortune 100** national bank as a residential loan officer. He was personally responsible for approximately $200 million (or more) in consumer direct sales in 3 years and recognized in 3 national sales campaigns.

As a natural progression derived from many of his various talents, skills, & life experiences, such as being a paralegal for a visually impaired (blind) attorney & legal analyst for a state agency, & related technical writing, editing, & evaluating written material, he began writing & assisting others in their endeavors as a technical publishing consultant. Paul G. Ellsworth has owned his own publishing advisory practice since 1999.

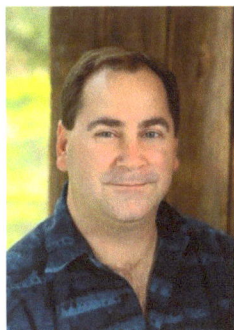

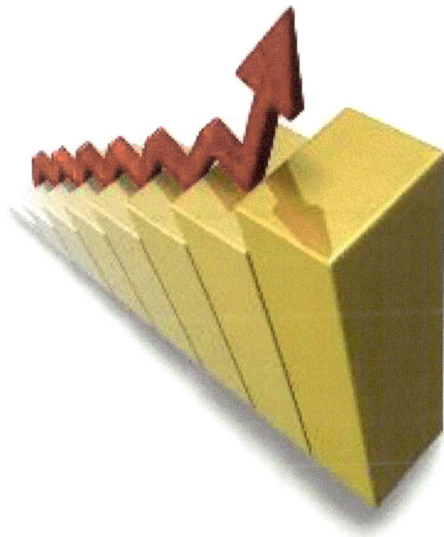

www.ingramcontent.com/pod-product-compliance
Lightning Source LLC
Chambersburg PA
CBHW041703210326
41598CB00007B/516